DISCOVER YOUR MESSAGE

DISCOVER YOUR MESSAGE

A 14-day guide to uncover your calling and find your niche as a writer, coach, or speaker

Jonathan Milligan

Copyright © 2023 by Jonathan Milligan

All rights reserved.

No portion of this book may be reproduced in any form without written permission from the publisher or author, except as permitted by U.S. copyright law.

This publication is designed to provide accurate and authoritative information in regard to the subject matter covered. It is sold with the understanding that neither the author nor the publisher is engaged in rendering legal, investment, accounting or other professional services. While the publisher and author have used their best efforts in preparing this book, they make no representations or warranties with respect to the accuracy or completeness of the contents of this book and specifically disclaim any implied warranties of merchantability or fitness for a particular purpose. No warranty may be created or extended by sales representatives or written sales materials. The advice and strategies contained herein may not be suitable for your situation. You should consult with a professional when appropriate. Neither the publisher nor the author shall be liable for any loss of profit or any other commercial damages, including but not limited to special, incidental, consequential, personal, or other damages. AI was used in the research & outlining of this book, but a human editor made editorial changes and humanly verified all citations and facts represented in the book.

Book Cover by Platform Growth Books

Illustrations by Jonathan Milligan

1st edition 2023

YOUR FREE GIFT

As a way of saying thanks for your purchase, we are offering a free companion online course called, *The Discover Your Message Accelerator Course.*

With this companion online course, you'll be able to fully implement all the exercises, worksheets, and checklists inside this book. To get free instant access, go to:

MarketYourMessage.com/discover-course

Purpose
(Your Strengths)

Passion
(Your Message)

People
(Your Audience)

The Ignite Your Message Framework

Inside the page of this book, you'll discover a powerful framework known as the Ignite Your Message Framework. To discover your message, you need clarity on three things: purpose (your strengths), people (your audience), and passion (your message).

Contents

Introduction		IX
1.	Day 1. The Ignite Your Message Framework	1
2.	Day 2. Finding Your Inner Drive	9
3.	Day 3. The Influencer Voice Assessment	19
4.	Day 4. Your One Word	28
5.	Day 5. Putting Your Purpose Together	35
6.	Day 6. The Egoic Label Exercise	41
7.	Day 7. The Audience Filter Scorecard	52
8.	Day 8. Discovering Your Audience's Goals	64
9.	Day 9. Finding Your Audience's Passions	73
10.	Day 10. Uncovering Your Audience's Struggles	81
11.	Day 11. How Will I Attract Them?	91
12.	Day 12. How Will I Capture Them?	102
13.	Day 13. How Will I Help Them?	110
14.	Day 14. Your Message in a Single Sentence	122
15.	The Journey of Discovering Your Message	132
16.	The Discover Your Message 14-Day Action Plan	134
Endnotes		152

Introduction

There are no extras.

You have a specific starring role to play. Inside the pages of this book, you'll uncover your unique calling and purpose.

As Richard Stearns, President of World Vision, says, "God created you intentionally to play a very specific role in his unfolding story. God didn't create any extras meant to just stand on the sidelines and watch the story unfold; he created players meant to be on center stage. And you will feel fully complete only when you discover the role you were born to play."[1]

You are about to discover a powerful fourteen-day self-discovery journey. Can your life change in just two short weeks? Yes, it can. Once you uncover your powerful purpose, the sky is the limit.

Have you ever felt like something was missing in your life? Like you were meant for something more but couldn't quite put your finger on it? And what if I said that you could uncover it in just 14 days?

Inside these pages, you'll embark on a powerful journey of self-discovery. Let this book be your guide to uncovering your gifts and finding your audience in 14 days or less. Following Richard Stearns, you're crafted for center stage, not merely to spectate from the sidelines.

It's time to take center stage and discover the role you were born to play. Are you ready for this life-changing journey?

Right now, you may feel lost, unfulfilled, and uncertain about your direction in life. You may have a nagging feeling that there's something more you're meant to do, but you need to figure out what that is and how to find it. You may feel stuck in your writing, coaching, or speaking career, not creating the impact you know you can. You may be experiencing frustration, anxiety, and even despair as you search for your place in the world.

But there is hope.

This book will guide you through a 14-day journey of self-discovery that will help you uncover your unique gifts and calling. By the end of this journey, you will clearly understand your purpose and how to share it with the world.

Through personal stories, valuable exercises, and expert advice, you can spot and conquer your obstacles. You will no longer feel stuck or uncertain about your path in life. Instead, this book will empower you to take action and confidently pursue your dreams.

So if you are tired of feeling unfulfilled and unsure of your place in the world, this book is for you. It's time to take control of your life and discover the unique role that you were born to play.

By the end of this 14-day journey, you will experience a powerful transformation. Here are some of the benefits you can expect to gain:

- Discover your unique gifts and talents and how to use them to impact the world.

- Gain clarity on your purpose and calling and how to align your life with it.

- Learn how to communicate your message to your audience effectively.

- Develop a clear plan of action to achieve your goals and make your dreams a reality.

- Build confidence in yourself and your writing, coach, or speaker abilities.

- Overcome the obstacles holding you back and step into your full potential.

- Join a welcoming community of individuals who share your interest in self-discovery and offer support along the way.

- Experience a renewed sense of purpose, fulfillment, and joy in your life and work.

Don't settle for a mediocre life.

You were created for greatness, and it's time to step into your full potential.

I understand the struggle of feeling stuck in a career or life that doesn't fulfill you. For years, I worked in a job that drained my energy and passion, leaving me feeling unfulfilled and longing for something more. But, after going through a similar self-discovery journey that I'm sharing with you in this book, I found my true calling as a writer, coach, and speaker.

I've spent years helping people unearth their unique talents and find their purpose, making a real difference in their lives. This book culminates my years of experience, research, and coaching expertise.

I wrote this book to help guide you on your journey of self-discovery and purpose. I want to help you unlock your full potential and find the confidence to pursue the life and career that aligns with your passions and values. With this book, you'll have the tools to take the first steps toward living the life you were meant to lead.

Are you ready to discover your unique calling and purpose?

Are you ready to uncover your gifts and find your audience?

Are you ready to transform your life and finally step into the role you were born to play?

If so, turn the page and start this powerful fourteen-day journey together. It's time to uncover your powerful purpose and impact the world. I can't wait to see the transformation that will take place in your life. Let's go!

1
Day 1. The Ignite Your Message Framework

Did you know that according to Forbes, 53% of people are unhappy at work?[2] It's no secret that numerous people journey through life feeling unfulfilled, unsure of their true purpose, or unable to connect with the right audience.

Imagine creating a life and career where your unique abilities flourish, directly impacting those who need your help and genuinely igniting your passion for helping others.

In this chapter, we'll take a transformative journey through a powerful framework I've developed called the Ignite Your Message Framework. This innovative method brings an end to aimless pursuits and instead allows your true purpose to shine.

At its core, the Ignite Your Message Framework revolves around three foundational pillars: purpose, people, and passion. Within the upcoming sections of this chapter, we'll provide you with an in-depth overview of these cornerstones and guide you through their powerful interplay.

With this knowledge, you can finally begin living the life you've always desired, creating an impact in your chosen field, and leaving your unique mark on the world. So, let's embark on this exciting adventure as we uncover the life-changing power of the Ignite Your Message Framework.

Day 1. The Ignite Your Message Framework

Let's start with an important question:

How do you discover your message?

Discovering your message may seem like a daunting task, but fear not. By leveraging the Ignite Your Message Framework and its three foundational pillars, you can unlock the true essence of what you want to share with the world. It all begins with the purpose, people, and passion in your life.

To successfully discover your message, follow these essential steps:

1. Identify Your Purpose: Start by examining your unique gifts, talents, and abilities. These natural strengths can provide crucial insights into how you can best serve others, whether it's through teaching, writing, speaking, or countless other avenues. Take the time to evaluate your past experiences, triumphs, and challenges, and understand how they have shaped your strengths. Be honest about your talents and how to use them to impact others positively. As you dive further into the book, we will introduce some helpful exercises to help you find your purpose.

2. Connect with Your People: Through purpose, you'll have a much clearer understanding of who you are and what you have to offer. The next vital step is connecting with the right audience – those who genuinely need your unique gifts. Carefully analyze and define your target audience, considering age, interests, location, and pain points. Your ability to empathize and understand your audience's needs, wants, and desires is fundamental to establishing meaningful connections and providing valuable guidance.

3. Fuel Your Passion: Finally, focus on your passion – the deep-seated drive that fuels your desire to help solve your audience's problems. Consider the topics, issues, or ideas that profoundly resonate with you and your audience.

This passion will drive your message, empowering you to create powerful, engaging content that supports your audience. It's essential to remain open to evolving your passion over time, as growth and change are natural parts of any journey.

By exploring these three critical aspects – your purpose, people, and passion – you'll be well on your way to discovering your unique message. The Ignite Your Message Framework serves as the vehicle on this transformative journey, guiding you to create a harmonious blend of your strengths, audience insights, and personal drive. Each element feeds into the others, making investing time and effort into understanding and nurturing all three pillars crucial.

Only then will you unveil the powerful message within you, allowing you to create a lasting impact and leave a memorable legacy. The whole premise of this book is based on the Ignite Your Message Framework. The better you understand this concept, the easier it will be to discover your message.

Let's simplify the three Ignite Your Message Framework parts even further.

- Purpose – How You Help.
- People – Who You Help.
- Passions – What You Help with.

Step 1. Purpose (Your Strengths)

All right, now that we've covered the basics of getting started with discovering your message, let's turn our attention to purpose. If you already know your strengths, you can skip ahead. Still, even if you understand your unique abilities well, I encourage you to stick around for some valuable exercises that might surprise you.

As I was going through my journey of self-discovery, I realized that I was only okay with many things. But what was my superpower? What was it about my style that attracted people to me? Through trial and error, I developed different exercises and tools to help others identify their strengths, whether they were writers, speakers, teachers, or coaches.

In an upcoming chapter, you'll walk through a series of exercises to discover your unique superpower and hone in on the main thing that makes you stand out. By the time you finish, you'll have an adjective word to describe how you show up best, along with a way of doing it - your influencer voice.

For example, my superpower is being a teacher. That doesn't mean I can't be a writer or a speaker, but primarily, my business centers around me being a teacher. Through an exercise you'll learn, I discovered that the word that best describes me is "practical" or "resourceful." I create tools to take complex topics and break them down into bite-sized courses to help my audience progress.

By the end of this section, you'll have discovered your unique superpower and know the two words that will help you lean into serving your audience better. So, take your time, go through the exercises, and get ready to discover your hidden superpower.

Step 2. People (Your Audience)

Once you understand how you show up best and have discovered your unique superpower, embracing your individuality is the next crucial step in building a business around your message. This is what will help you stand out in the crowded marketplace. You need to be more of yourself – no one else can do that better.

Next, we will explore a proven process for finding your people.

You might already have a clear idea of your audience, but even if you do, I encourage you to go through this section, as it will help you define them on an even deeper level.

But if you need to figure out who your audience should be, don't worry. We have specific exercises to guide you in finding them. We can help you target the most relevant audience by narrowing down your options if you're attempting to reach multiple groups.

This section has two main parts: finding your audience and defining them. If you can define your audience well, everything else becomes easier – writing emails, crafting sales copy, making offers, and more. Knowing your audience's needs allows you to serve them better and build stronger relationships.

Treat this section with care and attention, as it will give you the clarity needed for the next steps in your journey. So, with that said, let's move on to step three.

Step 3. Passion (Your Message)

Now that we've discussed your purpose and understanding your audience, embracing your passion is the last vital component of this journey. Remember, these steps are sequential and build upon each other to help you create your message.

Your passion stems from your unique combination of natural talents, gifts, and skills; you can best serve others through these. So, let's dive into how to define and hone in on that passion.

When thinking about passion, don't let the word overwhelm you. Instead, consider who you want to serve for the next two to five years and what you want to help them with. And remember, your focus can evolve – my journey went from assisting CPAs to being the blogging guy to ultimately supporting authors, coaches, and speakers in building their audiences.

We aim to help you craft a one-sentence message encompassing your strengths, your audience, and what you help them with. This concise, powerful statement will provide clarity and purpose for your business. We have a straightforward process to guide you through defining your message.

Like the other sections, we will have exercises to help you find the right audience.

Discovering your message requires deep understanding and integrating the three pillars within the Ignite Your Message Framework: purpose, people, and passion. As explored in this chapter, this transformative journey begins with embracing your unique self and strengths, connecting with the right audience, and fueling your desire to serve others effectively.

As you embark on Day 1 of this 14-day challenge, your first exercise will help lay the foundation for your message:

Day 1 Exercise: Reflect on Your Purpose, People, and Passion

- Spend 5-10 minutes journaling about your unique strengths, talents, and abilities. How have you used these in the past to serve others?

- Brainstorm the ideal audience you wish to serve, considering their demographics, desires, pain points, and passions.

- List your areas of interest and expertise, and explore how they align with your audience's needs and your unique talents.

Keep this exercise at the forefront of your mind as you continue through the upcoming chapters, allowing it to guide you toward discovering your authentic message.

Day 1 Key Takeaways:

- Embrace your unique gifts to enhance your impact and better serve others.

- Define your audience, understanding their needs and desires to foster deep connections.

- Discover and nurture your passion, driving you to help others solve their pressing problems.

Now that you have experienced Day 1 of this 14-day journey, you are one step closer to uncovering your true message, creating impactful content, and standing out in the world. Embark confidently on this adventure, knowing that the Ignite Your Message Framework will guide you towards a fulfilling, purpose-driven life where your passion for helping others flourishes.

2
Day 2. Finding Your Inner Drive

In the Summer of 1987, I was an 11-year-old boy feeling bored despite being out of school. As the oldest of three boys, we all shared a common interest—sports cards. Whenever our father brought home a box of unopened cards, we would have a blast opening them up, hoping to be the ones to pull out the expensive rookie cards. But our love of sports cards didn't stop there.

As an entrepreneur, I wanted to take our passion for sports cards to the next level. That's where my grandfather came in, who owned three hardware stores in Northern Indiana. He taught us business lessons during the Summer to keep us out of trouble.

One day, I thought of selling sports cards in his store, and he was more than happy to help. My brothers and I set up a sports card show on Saturday in my grandfather's hardware store. We priced our cards and created an attractive display. To our surprise, our little card show was a hit! We ended up selling over $400 worth of cards that day, and that experience ignited my passion for entrepreneurship.

My early entrepreneurship story with sports cards shows how childhood interests hint at our life's calling. Just as my passion for selling sports cards revealed my entrepreneurial spirit, your tendencies can lead you to your unique path.

By utilizing tools such as the 4-Part Interest Grid, we can gain further insight into what we are naturally drawn toward. This understanding can lead to confident decisions, guiding us to a more purposeful and satisfying life. So, what are you naturally drawn toward? Let's find out together.

Day 2. Finding Your Inner Drive

To begin discovering our calling, we need to look inside ourselves first. We should look to our past, childhood, high school, college, and adult working life to find clues about what we have been naturally drawn to. As Richard Leider has said, "Inside each of us right now is a call waiting to be answered."[3]

Finding our calling is not a one-time event but a series of events that point us in a direction. Clarity comes from movement, and we must approach our work as a calling to find fulfillment. The 4-Part Interest Grid can help point us in the right direction.

The Interest Grid consists of four categories: The Doer, The Talker, The Manager, and The Thinker. Each category has its own unique traits, and by identifying which category we fit into, we can discover our calling.

If you had to choose from one of the four categories, which would you choose? The goal is not to get it 100% right but directionally right. We need to be decisive and go with our gut. If we are drawn to all four categories, we should ask ourselves which cup is the fullest. For me, it was "The Thinker."

This book is about making decisions, and we must be decisive to get the most out of our journey. We can always revisit the exercises in this book in the future to see where we end up. The key is to keep moving forward and discover our calling.

The journey to discovering your calling begins with a look inside yourself. Reflect on your past - childhood, high school, college, or working life - for clues about your natural attractions. By investigating what naturally interests you, you can start to reveal the path to fulfilling your purpose.

The Doer category is comprised of individuals who are task-driven, decisive and bent toward action. They thrive on working with people and have a sense of urgency.

Managers are detail-oriented analyzers and system-driven individuals. They excel in organizing, handling repetitive tasks, and maintaining a consistent work approach.

Talkers excel in persuasive communication, selling, influencing, and motivating others. They connect with people and thrive in communication-focused environments.

Thinkers are creative individuals who excel in idea generation and big-picture vision. They are dreamers, writers, and innovators naturally inclined to creativity.

Knowing our category offers valuable insights into our natural interests. It helps us make informed decisions about our career and life paths, leading to greater fulfillment and purpose in our work. Consider which category resonates with you, and let the 4-Part Interest Grid guide your calling discovery.

The Doer (Coach)

The Doer is someone who is work-driven and likes to take action. They are decisive and have a sense of urgency to get things done. They thrive on challenges and are motivated by overcoming obstacles. A Doer is the kind of person who jumps right into a task and is not afraid of making mistakes. They learn best by doing and can become frustrated if they sit still for too long. They prefer to work through people and may be natural leaders.

Doers often find themselves in jobs that require quick thinking, decision-making, and action. They may be drawn to sales, marketing, customer service, or project management careers. A Doer is comfortable with change and can adapt to new situations quickly. They are always looking for ways to improve and streamline their work processes. They are not content with the status quo and constantly seek new challenges and opportunities for growth.

If you identify as a Doer, you are likely motivated by achieving results and making an impact. You thrive in fast-paced environments and enjoy taking on new challenges.

You may find it difficult to sit still for long periods of time and prefer to work in roles that allow you to be up and moving around. Understanding your tendencies as a Doer aligns your career choices with your strengths and interests.

Tony Robbins is an excellent example of a coach who embodies the Doer style. Tony's high-energy and action-oriented coaching style urges clients to take decisive action. He is always focused on results and getting things done, a hallmark of the Doer style.

Tony's coaching methodology is all about taking massive action and getting results. He uses powerful, straightforward language and techniques to motivate his clients to take action, even when they might not feel ready. His coaching sessions are designed to be intense and fast-paced, which keeps his clients engaged and motivated.

Whether with executives or entrepreneurs, Tony helps clients achieve goals through decisive action. His coaching style is perfect for those who thrive on activity and want to see immediate results in their lives.

Tony Robbins is an excellent example of a coach who embodies the Doer style. Tony is about massive action and results. His high-energy coaching suits those who want immediate outcomes and enjoy action.

The Manager (Teacher)

The Manager is detail-oriented, loves analyzing systems, and continuously seeks ways to improve them. They are methodical in their approach to work and thrive on repetitive tasks that require consistency. They are known for their organizational skills and are great at tracking numbers and figures.

Managers make great leaders in businesses and organizations as they know how to create structure and order. Managers excel in roles involving team management, development, and budget-conscious task completion.

Managers excel in pinpointing inefficiencies and implementing system improvements. Managers flourish in project management, where precision and a systematic approach are essential.

As a Manager, you'll gravitate towards careers related to problem-solving and system creation. You excel in roles responsible for organizing and managing resources, people, or projects.

By maintaining the right mindset and putting in the necessary effort, you have the potential to achieve success in your writing or coaching business.

One example of an online course creator who embodies the traits of a Manager on the 4-Part Interest Grid is Marie Forleo. She takes a system-driven approach to creating and marketing online courses.

Forleo emphasizes systems and processes, evident in the content and programs she offers. She also uses data and metrics to make informed decisions about improving her courses and reaching a wider audience. Additionally, she excels at breaking down complex concepts into manageable steps.

Overall, Forleo's approach to online course creation reflects the traits of a Manager on the 4-Part Interest Grid. Her detail-focused approach and emphasis on systems have driven her business success.

The Talker (Speaker)

The Talker is a unique style that embodies the art of communication. These individuals excel in verbal communication, engaging and influencing others effectively. Talkers are natural salespeople, skilled negotiators, and exceptional presenters. They thrive on being in front of an audience and can speak on various topics with confidence and ease.

Talkers have a way with words and can convey complex ideas simply and clearly. They are persuasive and can motivate and inspire others to take action. They can easily read the room and adjust their message to connect with their audience. Talkers excel in communication and active listening, fostering strong relationships.

One excellent example of a Talker is Simon Sinek, a renowned author and motivational speaker.

Sinek is a talented speaker who has inspired millions through books and TED talks. With his knack for simplifying complex ideas, Sinek is a sought-after keynote speaker, embodying the Talker style.

The Thinker (Writer)

The Thinker style is all about big-picture thinking, creativity, and innovation. People who fit this category are often visionaries, dreamers, and idea generators. They thrive on new concepts and enjoy exploring what could be. They are often drawn to artistic pursuits like writing, painting, or music.

For an author or blogger, the Thinker style is a perfect fit. They love exploring ideas and delving deep into a topic to create a unique perspective.

They are driven by curiosity and constantly seek new ways to share their ideas and thoughts. They may spend hours pondering over a single sentence, trying to find the right word or phrase to convey their message.

An example of a blogger who fits the Thinker style is Maria Popova, the creator of Brain Pickings.

Maria's blog merges art, science, and philosophy in accessible yet thought-provoking ways. As a prolific writer, Maria researches diverse subjects, crafting insightful content.

Another example is Austin Kleon, author of "Steal Like an Artist" and other books. He is known for his innovative approach to creativity, using a mix of words and images to convey his message. Austin's work is highly original, constantly exploring new ways to express his ideas. Austin is a great example of the Thinker type.

Which One Most Describes You?

Remember, we can exhibit qualities in all four areas of the Messenger Interest Grid. I would even say that we can also develop skills in all four areas over time. But for now, I'd like you to choose the primary one that best describes you.

Here is a summary for each of the Doer, Manager, Talker, and Thinker styles:

The Doer (Coach)	The Talker (Speaker)
Work through people	Persuasive communication
Task-driven	Natural at Selling
Bent toward action	Natural at Speaking
Decisive	Influences Others
Works with urgency	Motivates Others
The Manager (Teacher)	**The Thinker (Writer)**
Detail-oriented	Creative
Analyzer	Big picture visionary
Systems driven	Innovative
Organized	Dreamer
Likes routines	Idea creator

Remember the story I shared about my childhood sports card business? That experience ignited a fire within me that still burns brightly today. It was a defining moment. It revealed my natural inclination toward entrepreneurship, creativity, and innovation.

As you reflect on your own life, think about those moments that made you feel alive, engaged, and fulfilled. What were you doing? Who were you with? What skills were you utilizing? These are all clues to your natural talents and interests.

The next chapter will dive deeper into identifying our strengths and unique abilities. But before we move on, take a moment to appreciate the journey you're embarking on. Discovering your calling is a process, not a destination, and it's okay if you don't have all the answers right away.

Remember, inside each of us is a call waiting to be answered. As we progress on our journey, we will unveil our true potential and uncover the distinctive role we are meant to fulfill in this world.. So, please take a deep breath, trust the process, and let's continue on this journey together.

Day 2 Exercise: Complete the Messenger Interest Grid Assessment

Take the 4-Part Interest Grid assessment to determine your primary category. It will help you explore your natural interests and potential calling.

Day 2 Key Takeaways:

- The 4-Part Interest Grid comprises the Doer, Manager, Talker, and Thinker.
- Each category has unique traits and helps identify our calling.
- The Doer is task-driven and decisive, while the Manager is detail-oriented and systems-driven.
- The Talker persuades and communicates skillfully, while the Thinker is creative and visionary.
- By identifying which category we fit into, we can discover

our calling.

- It's essential to make a decision and go with our gut.

- We can revisit the exercises in this book to see where we end up in the future.

- Clarity comes from movement, and we must approach our work as a calling to find fulfillment.

3
Day 3. The Influencer Voice Assessment

It was my first in-person event, and I was nervous.

Sixteen people had paid over $5,000 to attend a 2-day workshop with me. The pressure to over-deliver was intense. I was so unsure of myself that I partnered with another influencer 50/50 on the workshop proceeds. I took a deep breath and walked into the room. The mastermind retreat ended up being a huge success. But the greatest win I received was not the income but from the information. The attendees were smart and asked great questions. They pushed me and challenged me in a good way.

One of the themes that came up over and over again was about finding their unique influencer voice. They didn't use those words, but they said things like:

- I hate blogging. Building an audience is important, but the blinking cursor and the blank page taunt me.
- Do I have to become a speaker? I prefer to stay home and write blog posts and books.
- I'm so tired of writer's block. But if you put me in front of a camera and give me a topic, I can talk for hours.

This was a bit puzzling to me at first. Here I have a room full of influencers; some love to write, some hate to write, some love to speak, and some hate to speak. How can I serve these people when they are so different? As I pondered this dilemma for the next few months, I came up with an idea.

Sometimes the best ideas come from asking good questions. I asked myself, "How come there is no personality test to help influencers discover if they are more of a writer, speaker, teacher, or coach? That was the day I created the first version of the Influencer Voice Assessment.

Day 3. The Influencer Voice Assessment

At the time of this writing, it's been six years since that first workshop. Since then, thousands of influencers have taken the Influencer Voice Assessment. Over the years, we've tweaked and improved the assessment for maximum clarity and results. The goal of this exercise is to help you determine where your primary motivation lies.

Below you will find our 32-question assessment. As you take the assessment, take your time with each statement. Go with your first response to the statement. There are no right and wrong answers. There is no pass or fail grade. Your answers are your answers. If you struggle with the assessment, take it with someone who knows you best. For a free online version, go to marketyourmessage.com/quiz.

Read each statement and give it one of the following ratings: 1 (Never), 2 (Rarely), 3 (Sometimes), 4 (Very Often), and 5 (Always). Let's do the first two statements together, and then you can do the rest.

The Influencer Voice Assessment

	1 Never	2 Rarely	3 Sometimes	4 Very Often	5 Always
1. I am naturally drawn toward action.					
2. I enjoy helping others solve problems.					

The first statement reads, "I am naturally drawn toward action." If you quickly jump into action before your questions are answered, you are a 5 (Always). If you tend to overthink and do a lot of research first, then you are a 1 (never). If you are somewhere in between, choose between 2-4.

The second statement reads, "I enjoy helping others solve problems." If you love to get personally involved with people with problems (and you don't mind getting messy), place a 5. If getting personally involved with people to help them overcome their problems drains you (instead of energizing you), then put a 1. By the way, placing a 1 does not make you a bad person. It just means you have other strengths.

Okay, now you are ready to answer the other 30 questions independently. Begin!

	1 Never	2 Rarely	3 Sometimes	4 Very Often	5 Always
3. I am energized by the opportunity to influence a live audience.					
4. I give shape to ideas by linking them to feelings and thoughts.					
5. I enjoy taking a complex subject and creating my own simple outline.					
6. I prefer to work in groups and teams over working alone.					
7. I am an avid reader and learner.					
8. I love creating my own worksheets and tools.					
9. When I plan, I see both the vision and the details of a project or goal.					
10. I am a natural storyteller.					
11. I work best when I can process ideas and concepts through writing first.					
12. When in a group, I have a keen awareness of whether people are engaged.					
13. I tend to be more at ease when teaching a larger group, rather than a small group of people.					
14. When I learn something new, I tend to want to share it with others around me.					
15. I don't mind being a bit vulnerable if necessary.					
16. I love to connect the dots on a subject and come up with an innovative solution.					
17. When it comes to completing projects, I tend to be task-driven.					

	1 Never	2 Rarely	3 Sometimes	4 Very Often	5 Always
18. Parties and people energize me.					
19. My personality tends toward introversion, but I still have a high need to influence others.					
20. I desire to be as free as possible from social demands.					
21. I enjoy one-on-one and small group interaction over working in large groups.					
22. I am energized by spending time reading and thinking.					
23. I love to learn all I can on a topic and then create my own summary or application.					
24. I prefer to influence, persuade, and motivate others in person.					
25. I tend to speak the truth in love rather than staying silent in order to avoid conflict.					
26. The idea of teaching a group of people every month excites me.					
27. I am naturally perceptive and curious.					
28. I like to use a sense of humor as a way to connect with others.					
29. I am energized by the thought of hosting an hour-long webinar to a large audience.					
30. I often see the hidden potential in others before they do.					
31. I value creative expression and deep thinking.					
32. I prefer to not be overscheduled on my calendar.					

Time to Score the Assessment

Using the scorecard below, record each score to the corresponding question. For example, if you wrote down 2 (Rarely) for question number one, write "2" next to question 1 below. Do the same for all thirty-two questions. Once you've recorded your answers to all the questions, add your score for each column.

Coach Score	Speaker Score	Writer Score	Teacher Score
1. =	3. =	4. =	5. =
2. =	6. =	7. =	8. =
9. =	10. =	11. =	13. =
17. =	12. =	16. =	14. =
21. =	15. =	20. =	19. =
25. =	18. =	22. =	23. =
27. =	24. =	31. =	26. =
30. =	28. =	32. =	29. =
Total:	Total:	Total	Total

Congratulations, you nailed a perfect score!

Okay, that was a bad joke. Remember, there is no pass or fail. This assessment helps you to identify where your core motivations lie. Don't be discouraged if "writer" was low on the assessment. It has nothing to do with competency.

As your business grows, I want you to develop skills in all four influencer voices. For now, we are going to lean into our primary influencer voice. Now, let's dive into why I had you take the assessment in the first place.

The Four Influencer Voices Explained

Writer, speaker, teacher, and coach. Those are the four primary ways anyone with a message can influence an audience. I'm a visual person, so I created the Messenger Product Map. This tool will help you see the big picture of where we are going with this.

The Messenger Product Map

Writer	Speaker
Kindle Books Physical Books Audiobooks	Keynote Talks Live Events Workshops
Teacher	**Coach**
Online Courses Membership Site Paid Webinar Series	1-on-1 Coaching 4–6 Week Group Coaching 1-Year Paid Mastermind

Writer and teacher are displayed on the left side of the map. Speaker and coach on the right side. Also, notice the multiple income streams that can be created for each influencer's voice. For writers, there are three income streams— Kindle books, physical books, and audiobooks. For teachers, there are three income streams—online courses, membership sites, and a paid webinar series. For speakers, there are three income streams—paid keynote talks, live events, and workshops.

For a coach, there are three income streams—1-on-1 coaching, 4-6 week group coaching, and a 1-year paid mastermind. The point of all this is for you to realize you have many ways to get paid for your message. The Messenger Product Map gives you twelve income stream ideas for a single message. But creating all twelve at once is a recipe for disaster.

The primary goal for today is for you to select one of the four influencer voices. Decide to stick with your chosen influencer voice until you make your first (or next) $1,000 or more in your business. In the next chapter, I'll show you how to combine who you are with what you do.

As we wrap up Chapter 3, it's essential to reflect on the importance of understanding your unique influencer voice. Identify your key motivation. It can guide you to success. You'll use your strengths. You'll impact your audience powerfully.

For Day 3, let's put your newfound knowledge into action with an exercise that will bring your influencer voice to life.

Day 3 Exercise: Discover Your Primary Influencer Voice

- Finish the Influencer Voice Assessment. It reveals your key motivation. Are you a writer, speaker, teacher, or coach?

- Consider how leaning into this primary voice can shape and strengthen your message and impact on your audience.

- Develop a plan to focus on your primary influencer voice for your first (or next) $1,000 earned in your business.

Day 3 Key Takeaways:

- Knowing your influencer voice is vital. It creates an audience connection.

- Focusing on your core motivation will pave the way for a faster income and impact journey.

- Remember that you can develop skills in all four influencer voices as your business grows.

Ready to move to the next chapter? Keep your influencer voice ready. Marry who you are with what you do. Unlock more influence and success in your message journey. See you on the next page!

4
Day 4. Your One Word

To find your purpose, we need to uncover what's unique about you. There are things you do that come naturally to you. To be an effective writer, coach, or speaker, we need to find where our magic lies.

Author Brian Dixon says, "What's ordinary for you is magic to others."[4] Once you uncover this (and believe this to be true), you'll know how you best show up in the world. For example, my superpower is to be a practical, resourceful teacher. That's how I can show up best for others.

In the Summer of 2022, I took a 30-day Sabbatical. I've been observing this practice for years. It helps me unplug from my work, spend more time with family, and let my team fully own my business. During my sabbatical, I rest, vacation, and dive into hobbies I normally don't make time for.

During my 2022 Sabbatical, I dove back into sports cards. I've been collecting sports cards since I was a kid in the late eighties and nineties. Since I have an extensive collection, I started selling some of the more valuable cards on eBay.

I had so much fun learning a new business model. I set up systems for each part of the business. I had a system of photography, listing auctions, inventory, and shipping. How did I know how to do all that if I had never done it before? I leaned into my strength of being resourceful.

A part of being resourceful is consuming large amounts of information and then distilling it into its simplest parts. Within a week, I had a complete eBay business system that I could run for thirty minutes or less daily.

Why am I telling you all of this? My parents, who recently retired, learned what I was doing and wondered if they could do the same with books. So, I went and stayed with them for a few days and helped them set up their business systems for their book business on eBay.

Within thirty days, they had over five hundred books listed on eBay and consistently sold two to five books per day. All I did was lean into what I believe my purpose to be, which is to be a practical, resourceful teacher. I want the same for you.

Day 4. Your One Word

Do you want to make a positive impact on the lives of others? One of the best ways to do that is by showing up for people in ways that highlight your unique strengths. But how do you know what those strengths are?

Often, it takes input from others to help us see ourselves more clearly. In this chapter, we'll explore why it's crucial to discover how we best show up for others and how adjectives help us recognize our inherent gifts.

Discovering your unique strengths allows you to make a real difference in the lives of those around you. Understanding your "one word" is essential, as it represents the core of your strengths and can serve as a guiding force in your life.

The following three things happen once you uncover your one word:

Unlocks Your Potential

You unlock your true potential when you understand the essence of your strengths – your one word. You can focus on what you naturally excel at rather than spreading yourself thin by trying to excel in every area. Clarity boosts your work, relationships, and personal life. It empowers you to have a more significant impact on others.

Builds Confidence and Authenticity

Identifying your one-word also boosts your self-confidence. You'll feel more empowered and energized with a clear understanding of your strengths. Self-awareness fosters authentic connections, building genuine, respectful relationships.

Gives Your Work Meaning

Once you understand how you can add value to others, it gives your work meaning. You can have the confidence to know exactly how you can contribute value to a client, company, or business.

How to Discover Your One Word with the Help of Others

One way to uncover your one word is to seek honest feedback from friends, family, or colleagues. Request them to describe you using adjectives that reveal your unique gifts and strengths.

Reflect on the feedback you receive and look for recurring themes. These insights will help you pinpoint your one word and recognize how it shows up in your life.

Applying Your One Word to Your Life

Once you have identified the one word that represents your strengths, it's time to apply it in your daily life. Use your one word in your career, relationships, and hobbies. Impact others by expressing your one word. Focusing on your one word grows you and allows for authenticity. You will build trust-based connections.

Knowing your one word is vital. It boosts your impact and brings your best forward. It can help you hone in on your strengths. Maximize your potential. Create authentic bonds with your audience. Today's exercise is called the one-word exercise. To complete this exercise, you'll need the help of other people. A friend once told me, "It's hard to read the label when you're inside the bottle." To discover what your superpower is, you'll need an outside perspective.

It starts with identifying five people who know you best. This could be a spouse, close friend, sibling, or coworker. But it should be the five people who know you best. They've spent lots of time with you. Once you have your five names, you can complete the Unique Gifts Inventory List.

The Unique Gifts Inventory List

Below you'll find over sixty-five of people's most common positive traits. The goal is not for you to see how many of the sixty-five positive traits you have. Rather, finding the one superpower you do well is the goal.

The exercise works best when we involve the input of other people. There are two ways you can approach this exercise. First, you can just ask them to share the five words that describe you best. This will allow for open-ended responses. However, to get a higher response rate, you may want to send them the list of sixty-five traits below. People are busy and less likely to procrastinate if you make it easier for them.

Send this list to your five people and ask them the following question:

If you could describe me using five words, what would you choose from this list?

Academic-Based	Decisive	Idealistic	Perceptive
Achievement Driven	Deliberate	Imaginative	Persistent
	Detail-oriented	Independent	Persuasive
Accepting	Determined	Influential	Positive
Accurate	Diplomatic	Innovative	Practical
Adaptable	Disciplined	Insightful	Proactive
Adventurous	Dynamic	Introspective	Realistic
Aggressive	Easygoing	Joyful	Resourceful
Analytical	Empathetic	Kind	Supportive
Articulate	Energetic	Knowledgeable	Strategic
Calm	Enthusiastic	Logical	Sympathetic
Carefree	Focused	Loving	Tenacious
Caring	Generous	Methodical	Thorough
Charismatic	Grounded	Motivational	Traditional
Confident	Helpful	Organized	Versatile
Courageous	Humorous	Patient	Visionary
Creative			Witty

If you want a one-page PDF version of this list, go to marketyourmessage.com/inventory. Once you have the PDF, email it to your top five or attach it to a text or Facebook message.

Once you collect five words from each person, look for overlapping words. Although some of the words may not be exact, are they similar in some way? How do they overlap? Then, look for a one-word summary that fits you (and one that you like).

Next, frame and display that word in some way. You need to champion yourself. You have a powerful voice and service to offer the world. The good news is you don't have to be like other successful people. Just be you. And the more you lean into being you, the more you'll stand out.

My wife took a cool rock we found while hiking the Appalachian Trail and decoupaged the word "resourceful" on the rock. The rock still sits on a shelf in my office today. It's a constant reminder that I have value to add to others.

Once you've found your one word, celebrate it.

It's what is changeless about you.

Your career will change. Your jobs will change. But your purpose always remains.

You can throw me into any context, career, or job, but I'll always gravitate to my practical, resourceful superpower. The same is true for you, my friend. Fully embracing what's changeless about you will settle you and guide you to success.

Embracing your unique superpower by identifying your one word is a game-changer in how you show up for others and create a lasting impact. The Influencer Voice Assessment helps widen your understanding of your purpose.

As we move forward to day four, let's tackle the essential exercise that will set the stage for unlocking your powerful message:

Day 4 Exercise: Find Your One Word

- Compile a list of the five people who know you best.
- Share the Unique Gifts Inventory List with them, asking them to choose five words that best describe you.
- Look for overlapping or similar words and settle on a one-word summary that resonates with your unique self.
- Embrace and celebrate your one-word summary – this is your superpower.

Day 4 Key Takeaways:

- Your unique superpower is the driving force behind your success and impact.
- Understanding and embracing your one word not only refines your message but also provides guidance through life's inevitable changes.
- Seeking input from others can offer valuable insights into finding the essence of your innate strengths.

With your one-word summary, you are ready to combine this newfound understanding with your influencer voice to create a compelling, impactful presence in your field. So, let's dive into the next phase of this exciting journey!

5
Day 5. Putting Your Purpose Together

In 1961, President John F. Kennedy announced a bold goal for the United States: to put a man on the moon and bring him safely back to Earth by the end of the decade.

At the time, the technology to accomplish such a feat did not exist, and many experts doubted it could be achieved. But Kennedy's vision inspired the nation, and within just eight years, NASA successfully accomplished the mission.[5]

Its technical expertise and ability to rally around a clear purpose allowed NASA to accomplish this seemingly impossible task.

They knew exactly what they were working towards and why it was important. Similarly, as authors and coaches, it's essential to clearly understand our purpose and the problems we aim to solve for our audience.

In this chapter, we'll explore how to define our purpose and narrow down the challenges our audience faces so we can create products and services that truly make a difference.

You'll be able to define your strengths using just two words. The good news is that you've already done the hard work of defining your "one word" and taking the Influencer Voice assessment.

Day 5. Putting Your Purpose Together

Your purpose is not a thing, it's something inside of you, and that's what makes it awesome.

Richard Leider says, "Unlocking one's calling requires an inward journey. Each one of us has unique potential — distinct, innate gifts — with which to serve the world. These gifts provide us with a source of identity in the world, but until we connect who we are with what you do, that source remains untapped."[6]

Today, we will define your purpose in just two words and connect who you are with what you do. So, let's jump into the exercise of putting your purpose together.

Step 1. Your One Word

Step one of putting your purpose together is to write down your one word from the one-word exercise. This exercise helps you to uncover your unique gift and define your purpose. Getting it down to one word is important, even if you're unsure. This one word is the foundation of your brand, and it should be something that you are passionate about and that comes naturally to you.

If you haven't done the one-word exercise, take the time to do it. Many successful entrepreneurs and business leaders have used this exercise, which can help you gain clarity and focus. In fact, according to business coach and author Evan Carmichael, "The one-word exercise is the most powerful tool you have in your arsenal to become the best version of yourself and build a successful business."[7]

Once you have one word, it's time to apply it and progress through this journey. Don't worry about being perfect or having all the answers right away. This journey is about discovery and growth, and making mistakes along the way is okay. Remember, your purpose is not something out there; it's something inside of you. By embracing your unique gift and applying it to your business, you can achieve success and make a difference in the lives of others.

Step 2. Your Primary Influencer Voice

We have also walked through how to uncover your influencer voice. This is the voice that you naturally gravitate towards and excel in. Understanding this is important because it will guide how you communicate and connect with your audience.

According to a study by Influence & Co, 81% of business decision-makers trust blog advice.[8] This highlights the importance of being a writer influencer voice. On the other hand, 66% of consumers trust advertisements, highlighting the importance of being a speaker influencer voice.

It's important to note that your primary influencer voice can be different from your profession or job title. For example, you may work in marketing but have a primary influencer voice of a coach, which means you naturally excel in guiding and supporting others.

Identifying your main influencer voice is crucial to effectively connecting with your audience and establishing a prosperous business. As Simon Sinek said, "People don't buy what you do; they buy why you do it."[9] Your primary influencer voice is key to communicating your "why" and attracting your ideal audience.

So, please take a moment to circle your primary influencer voice and reflect on how it aligns with your one word. Are there any synergies or conflicts? How can you leverage your primary influencer voice to serve your audience better and build a successful business? These are important questions to consider as you continue to uncover your purpose.

Step 3. Combining the Two Words

By taking your primary influencer voice and combining it with your one word, you can start to define your purpose in a more tangible way. This purpose will guide you in everything you do, from the content you create to your products and services.

It's important to remember that your purpose is not set in stone. As you grow and evolve, your purpose may shift or change altogether. However, having a clear purpose can help you stay focused and motivated as you pursue your goals.

Studies have shown that people with a strong sense of purpose are happier and more successful personally and professionally. According to the University of Michigan research, "people who derive meaning and purpose from their work tend to be more engaged, satisfied, and resilient, and they achieve higher levels of success."[10]

So reflect on your one-word and primary influencer voice, and see how they can be combined to define your purpose. With this clarity, you'll be better equipped to positively impact the world and achieve your goals.

The goal of this exercise is for you to walk away with two words that describe how you best show up for others. By fully embracing your gift, you can build an online business through online courses, membership sites, webinars, and more. That's precisely what a resourceful teacher would do. That's the power of discovering your unique gift.

One inspiring story from history is that of Beethoven, the famous composer and pianist. As a child, Beethoven was forced by his father to practice music for hours on end, hoping to create another child prodigy like Mozart. However, Beethoven's true passion was in creating his own music, and he often stayed up late at night composing pieces that he hoped would be performed on the grandest stages of Europe.

Despite his father's disapproval and his struggles with hearing loss, Beethoven pursued his unique gift of music composition. He focused on creating innovative and emotionally stirring music, which eventually led to his breakthrough in the world of music. Beethoven's compositions, such as his Symphony No. 9 and Piano Sonata No. 14, better known as the Moonlight Sonata, became iconic pieces that would shape the future of classical music.

Beethoven's legacy has endured for centuries due to his discovery and cultivation of his unique gift. His music still inspires and captivates audiences around the globe.

His unwavering dedication to pursuing his passion is a powerful example of the importance of identifying and nurturing one's unique talents.

You have a responsibility to share your gift. You're selfish if you don't. So, come up with your two words, get excited about the journey ahead, and get excited about where we're going.

Remember, what's ordinary for you is magic for others. You have a gift that other people don't have. Use it, steward it.

That's my challenge for you today. Go get those two words, and let's move on to the next day in the challenge.

Day 5 Exercise: Create Your Two-Word Purpose

Combine your one-word and primary influencer voice to create a clear and concise purpose statement.

Day 5 Key Takeaways:

- Discovering your gift is essential to finding your purpose.
- Your purpose is not a thing; it's already inside you.
- Your passions may change, but your purpose remains.
- Your purpose is how you show up best for others.
- Listing your one-word and primary influencer voice can help you uncover your purpose.

6

Day 6. The Egoic Label Exercise

Jane had a passion for cooking. She loved experimenting with different ingredients and creating unique and delicious dishes. After much thought, she decided to turn her passion into a business and become a chef.

Jane had to start from scratch and build her business from the ground up. The first step was to identify her specific audience. After researching, she found the egoic label index and discovered that her egoic label was a chef.

But simply identifying herself as a chef wasn't enough. She needed to narrow down her audience to a specific group. After some reflection, she focused on serving busy professionals who didn't have time to cook for themselves.

To better understand her audience, Jane went through the exercise of identifying the problems and challenges they faced. She discovered that most of her target audience needed more time to cook healthy meals and often resorted to fast food or takeout. She also found that many had specific dietary requirements, such as gluten-free or vegan.

Jane then identified the goals and aspirations of her target audience. She realized her clients wanted healthy, delicious food tailored to their dietary needs. They also wanted the convenience of having their meals prepared and delivered to them.

Next, Jane identified the demographics and psychographics of her target audience. She discovered that her clients were mostly in their 30s and 40s, worked high-stress jobs, and valued their health and wellness. They were also interested in trying new foods and exploring different cultures.

With this information, Jane could tailor her products and services to her specific audience. She created a meal delivery service that offered healthy and delicious meals that catered to various dietary requirements.

She also added a personal touch by including handwritten notes with each meal and providing recommendations for other healthy habits, such as exercise and self-care.

Focusing on serving a specific audience, Jane built a loyal customer base and established herself as an authority in the meal delivery service niche. Her business grew, and she eventually hired a team of chefs to help her with the increasing demand.

Ultimately, Jane's success resulted from her commitment to identifying and serving a specific audience. By understanding her client's needs, wants, and preferences, she created a business that resonated with them.

Now, it's your turn. Let's walk through a simple yet powerful exercise to help you narrow down your audience.

Day 6. The Egoic Label Exercise

Throughout the preceding chapters, we have emphasized the significance of understanding your strengths. It's time to move on to the next step, identifying your specific audience. It's important to realize that your audience is not everyone. You cannot help and serve everyone. It's essential to be specific about who you want to serve.

The egoic label exercise is one of the most powerful exercises to help you identify your audience. An egoic label is a self-label you give yourself because you like it.

For example, you could be an entrepreneur, a small business owner, an author, a blogger, a speaker, a chef, a counselor, or a corporate executive. But how do you come up with egoic labels in the first place?

To simplify things, I've developed an egoic label index with five categories: vocation, ownership, religion, identity type, and hobbies. The vocation category includes labels related to your work or profession.

Ownership labels are related to things that you own and are proud of. Religion labels are related to your religious beliefs. Identity-type labels relate to your identity, such as being a cancer survivor, a single mom, or a vegan. Hobbies labels are related to your hobbies or interests.

Categories	Examples of Egoic Labels	
Vocation	☐ Entrepreneur ☐ Small business owner ☐ Blogger ☐ Author ☐ Speaker ☐ CPA	☐ Corporate Executive ☐ Counselor ☐ Lawyer ☐ Chef ☐ _____ ☐ _____
Ownership	☐ Homeowner ☐ Dog owner ☐ Cat owner ☐ Renter ☐ Mac Owner ☐ PC Owner	☐ Honda owner ☐ iPhone User ☐ RV Owner ☐ Boat Owner ☐ _____ ☐ _____
Religion	☐ Jewish ☐ Christian ☐ Muslim ☐ Atheist ☐ Buddhist ☐ Mormon	☐ Jehovah's Witness ☐ Catholic ☐ Hindu ☐ Baptist ☐ _____ ☐ _____
Identity	☐ Stepmom ☐ Single men over 40 ☐ Divorced women ☐ Single mom ☐ Athlete ☐ Cancer survivor	☐ Vegan ☐ Working mom ☐ Stay-at-home mom ☐ Women over 50 ☐ _____ ☐ _____
Hobbies	☐ Hiker ☐ Marathon Runner ☐ Outdoorsman ☐ Golfer ☐ Hunter ☐ Sportscard collector	☐ Skier ☐ Gardener ☐ World Traveler ☐ Dancer ☐ _____ ☐ _____

I want you to take some time to find three to six egoic labels that you think would be a good group for you to serve. You can choose from the index I provided or research and find your own. These egoic labels should be a group you can relate to, or it's something you're interested in.

Once you have your egoic labels, the next step is to identify the specific audience within that group that you want to serve. For example, if you chose the egoic label of a small business owner, you need to identify the specific type of small business owner you want to serve. It could be a small business owner in the tech industry or a small business owner in the restaurant industry.

To help you identify your specific audience, you can use the following exercise:

1. Identify the problems and challenges that your chosen group faces. This will help you understand their pain points and their need for help.

2. Identify the goals and aspirations of your chosen group. This will help you understand what they want to achieve and what motivates them.

3. Identify the demographics of your chosen group, such as age, gender, income, location, education, and profession. This will help you understand their background and what they value.

4. Identify the psychographics of your chosen group, such as their beliefs, values, interests, and lifestyle. This will help you understand their personality and what they enjoy doing.

By going through these steps, you will be able to identify your specific audience and understand their needs, wants, and preferences. This will allow you to tailor your products and services to their specific needs, making it more likely that they will buy from you.

Let's look at each of these in more depth.

Identify the Problems and Challenges of Your Audience

When starting a business, it's essential to understand your target audience's problems and challenges. This will help you identify their pain points and what they need help with, allowing you to tailor your products and services to meet their specific needs.

By identifying your target audience's problems and challenges, you can create solutions that directly address their pain points. For example, if you're targeting busy professionals who don't have time to cook, you can offer meal delivery services that provide healthy and delicious meals, saving them time and effort.

Understanding the pain points of your target audience will also help you communicate with them more effectively. By speaking their language and addressing their problems, you can build a strong relationship with them and establish yourself as an authority in your niche. This, in turn, will increase their trust in your business and make them more likely to become loyal customers.

Identifying the problems and challenges of your target audience can be done through market research, surveys, or simply talking to potential customers. By gathering this information, you can gain valuable insights into their needs and wants and use this information to improve your products and services. Don't worry. In a future chapter, I'll show you how to easily identify the problems and challenges of your audience.

Uncover the Goals and Aspirations of Your Audience

Identifying the goals and aspirations of your chosen audience is a critical step in building a successful business. By understanding what your target audience wants to achieve and what motivates them, you can tailor your products and services to meet their needs and provide them with the solutions they're looking for.

When you understand the goals and aspirations of your target audience, you can communicate with them in a way that resonates with them and provides them with a sense of purpose. This can help you build a strong emotional connection with your audience, increasing their loyalty and trust in your business.

According to a survey by LinkedIn, 75% of people believe that having a sense of purpose is important for their well-being, and 73% of people who feel fulfilled and purposeful in their work are likelier to be happy.[11]

Understanding the goals and aspirations of your target audience can also help you differentiate your products and services from your competitors. By providing solutions that align with your audience's goals and motivations, you can set yourself apart from other businesses that may not fully understand the needs of their customers.

Identify the Demographics of Your Audience

Identifying the demographics of your chosen group is a critical step in building a successful business. By understanding their background and what they value, you can tailor your products and services to meet their specific needs and preferences.

Demographics include various characteristics of your target audience, such as age, gender, income, location, education, and profession. By identifying these demographics, you can gain valuable insights into the background and lifestyle of your target audience.

For example, if you're targeting women over 50, you might want to offer products and services that cater to their specific needs, such as skin care products for mature skin or health and wellness services that address age-related issues.

Another example would be if you're targeting young professionals in a major city, you might want to offer products and services that are convenient and tech-savvy, such as mobile apps that help with productivity or food delivery services that cater to busy schedules.

Understanding the demographics of your target audience can also help you tailor your marketing messages and communication style. For example, if you're targeting a younger audience, you might use social media platforms like Instagram or TikTok to reach them, whereas if you're targeting an older audience, you might use traditional marketing channels like print ads or email marketing.

Identifying the demographics of your target audience is a crucial step in building a successful business. By understanding their background and what they value, you can tailor your products and services to meet their specific needs and preferences and communicate with them in a way that resonates with them. This can increase their loyalty and trust in your business and help you stand out from your competitors.

Identify the Psychographics of Your Audience

Understanding the psychographics of your chosen group is just as important as identifying their demographics. By understanding their beliefs, values, interests, and lifestyle, you can better understand their personality and what motivates them. This information can help you tailor your products and services to their specific needs and preferences.

For example, consider a business that sells outdoor equipment. They identify their target audience as individuals who enjoy camping, hiking, and other outdoor activities.

By understanding the psychographics of this group, they discover that their customers value sustainability and eco-friendliness. They then adjust their marketing messages to focus on the environmentally friendly aspects of their products, such as using recycled materials and sustainable manufacturing practices.

Another example would be a business that offers fitness classes. They identify their target audience as individuals interested in health and wellness. By understanding the psychographics of this group, they discover that their customers are highly motivated by social connections and group activities. They then adjust their marketing messages to emphasize the social aspect of their classes and the community that they have created.

Understanding the psychographics of your target audience can also help you identify what type of content they enjoy and how they like to be communicated with. For example, if your target audience is highly interested in fashion and lifestyle, you might want to create visually appealing content that uses influencers to showcase your products.

On the other hand, if your target audience is highly analytical and detail-oriented, you might want to provide more technical information and case studies to showcase the value of your products.

Identifying the psychographics of your target audience is a crucial step in building a successful business. By understanding their beliefs, values, interests, and lifestyle, you can tailor your products and services to meet their specific needs and preferences. This can increase their loyalty and trust in your business and help you stand out from your competitors.

Remember, the more specific you can be with your audience, the more powerful your communication will be. By understanding your audience, you can speak their language, and you will be able to connect with them on a deeper level. This will help you build a strong relationship with them and establish yourself as an authority in your niche.

Nailing down your specific audience is crucial for the success of your business. By using the egoic label exercise and identifying your specific audience, you will be able to understand their needs and wants and tailor your products and services to their specific needs. This will help you build a strong relationship with your audience and establish yourself as an authority in your niche.

In a future chapter, we will dive deeper into how to uncover your audience's goals, passions, and struggles. I'll teach you my proven Audience GPS System that will bring everything together for you and help you better define your audience. You'll also discover how knowing your audience's GPS makes content creation a breeze.

Never again will you struggle with developing ideas for blog posts, podcasts, or Youtube videos. Stay tuned!

Day 6 Exercise: The Egoic Label Exercise

Complete the Egoic Label exercise and develop at least four egoic labels you might use to create a business.

Day 6 Key Takeaways:

- Identifying your specific audience is crucial for the success of your business.
- Use the egoic label exercise to find a self-label that you like.
- Narrow down your audience to a specific group to better understand their needs.

- Identify the problems and challenges that your target audience faces.

- Understand the goals and aspirations of your target audience.

- Know the demographics and psychographics of your target audience.

- Tailor your products and services to the specific needs of your target audience.

- Build a strong relationship with your audience by speaking their language.

7
Day 7. The Audience Filter Scorecard

In the late 1800s, Coca-Cola was just a small, regional soft drink company in the southern United States. The company's founder, John Pemberton, had created the drink as a medicine to treat headaches and other ailments.

However, when Pemberton passed away, his partner Asa Candler saw the potential to turn Coca-Cola into a national brand. He recognized that the drink had a unique taste and could appeal to a wider audience beyond just those seeking medical remedies.

Candler began marketing Coca-Cola as a refreshing and delicious soft drink. He focused on the company's unique flavor and its ability to quench thirst on hot summer days. He advertised in newspapers and on billboards, but his biggest breakthrough was in identifying his audience: young, urban, working-class Americans.

Candler realized that this audience was often overlooked by other soft drink companies, who were targeting wealthier customers. He saw an opportunity to appeal to a broader market and began advertising Coca-Cola as an affordable and refreshing beverage that anyone could enjoy.

Candler's strategy paid off. By the early 1900s, Coca-Cola was the most popular soft drink in the United States. The company's focus on its unique taste and affordability resonated with its audience and helped it to grow into the global brand that it is today.[12]

The story of Coca-Cola demonstrates the power of identifying your audience and tailoring your message to their needs and interests. By focusing on a specific audience and understanding their value, you can create a connection that will help your business thrive.

Day 7. The Audience Filter Scorecard

One successful entrepreneur, let's call her Sarah, used the audience filter scorecard to identify her dream customers and build her business around them. Sarah had always been passionate about fitness and had experience as a personal trainer. However, she wasn't sure which audience to focus on when building her online business. She tried marketing to everyone interested in fitness but found it difficult to connect with her audience.

That's when Sarah discovered the audience filter scorecard. She chose her top three egoic labels: "yoga enthusiast," "working mom," and "vegetarian." Sarah filled out the scorecard for each egoic label and found that "yoga enthusiast" scored the highest. She was passionate about yoga and had experience teaching it, so it was a natural fit. She started to create content and products specifically for yoga enthusiasts. She wrote articles on the benefits of yoga and how to incorporate it into a busy lifestyle.

She created a yoga video course for working moms who wanted to practice at home. And she designed a line of yoga clothes made with eco-friendly and sustainable materials for vegetarians. With a clear focus on her dream customers, Sarah's business began to grow. She built a community of loyal followers who were passionate about yoga and appreciated her expertise in the field. She even expanded her offerings to include live yoga classes and retreats.

Thanks to the audience filter scorecard, Sarah could identify her dream customers and build a business that truly resonated with them. Her success shows that choosing the right audience can make all the difference in building a successful business.

You should have completed the egoic label exercise from the previous day. If you haven't done it yet, please do it before moving forward. Now, we are going to take the next step in identifying your audience using the audience filter scorecard.

First, let's remove the emotional pressure of this exercise. Sometimes, we tend to overthink and put too much stress on ourselves when trying to identify our audience or dream customers. We will approach it logically using the audience filter scorecard to make it easier.

Start by choosing your top three to six egoic labels. These are the labels that define your identity and your interests. For example, if you chose "high school teacher," "Mac owner," and "golfer," write them down in the top six columns.

Next, answer the six questions in the scorecard for each egoic label. Don't overthink it; just read through it and give an honest answer.

The questions are as follows:

1. Do I enjoy learning about this egoic label?
2. Am I passionate about this egoic label?
3. Do I have experience or skills related to this egoic label?
4. Does this egoic label have a problem to solve?
5. Are other businesses earning money helping this egoic label?

6. Do I want to serve this egoic label?

Before you give yourself a rating on the six questions above, let's further explain each question. You will then complete the Audience Filter Scorecard at the end of the chapter.

Question 1. Do I Enjoy Learning about this Egoic Label?

The first question in the audience filter scorecard is, "Do I enjoy learning about this egoic label?" This question is important because it can help you determine whether you can create content and products that resonate with your audience. If you enjoy learning about your egoic label, you will be motivated to continue researching and creating related content. You will be curious about the latest trends and developments in the field, and you will be excited to share this knowledge with your audience.

On the other hand, if you don't enjoy learning about your egoic label, creating engaging content and products will be difficult. You may find it tedious or uninteresting to keep up with the latest developments in the field. This could lead to a lack of motivation and, ultimately, to a decline in your business. Choosing an egoic label you are genuinely interested in and passionate about is important. This will help you to stay motivated and engaged in your business, even when challenges arise. By enjoying learning about your egoic label, you will be able to create content and products that truly resonate with your audience and build a community of loyal followers who share your passion.

Question 2. Am I Passionate about this Egoic Label?

The second question in the audience filter scorecard is, "Am I passionate about this egoic label?" This question is essential because your passion can drive your business forward and inspire your audience. Passion is the fuel that keeps entrepreneurs going, even when things get tough. When you are passionate about your business, you are likelier to put in the extra effort and time to make it successful. You will be more motivated to create content and products that benefit your audience.

A great example of the power of passion is the story of Walt Disney. Disney was passionate about animation and storytelling from a young age. He founded his animation company, which eventually became the Walt Disney Company, with a vision to create a world of wonder and imagination. Disney's passion for animation inspired him to create classic characters like Mickey Mouse, Snow White, and Cinderella. His passion also drove him to innovate, creating groundbreaking animation techniques and technologies. Disney's passion for storytelling and animation was infectious, inspiring generations of people worldwide. Today, the Walt Disney Company is one of the most successful entertainment companies in the world, with a global audience spanning generations.

The story of Walt Disney shows that passion is a powerful force that can drive business success and inspire others. By choosing an egoic label that you are passionate about, you can create a business that truly resonates with your audience and builds a community of loyal followers who share your enthusiasm. Passion serves as a deep well for you to draw from. This is especially important in the beginning of your business before the income starts rolling in.

Question 3. Do I have experience or skills related to this egoic label?

The third question in the audience filter scorecard is, "Do I have experience or skills related to this egoic label?" This question is important because having experience and skills in your egoic label can help you to create valuable content and products for your audience.

A study by HubSpot found that businesses that blogged regularly had 126% more lead growth than those that didn't.[13] This highlights the importance of creating valuable content for your audience. You can create informative, helpful, and engaging content if you have experience and skills in your egoic label.

Having experience and skills in your egoic label also means you have a deeper understanding of your audience's needs and pain points. This can help you to create products and services that truly address their problems and provide value.

For example, let's say you are passionate about photography and have experience as a professional photographer. You could use this experience to create a course that teaches aspiring photographers how to take better photos. By leveraging your skills and experience, you can create a valuable, unique product that can help your audience achieve their goals.

In conclusion, having experience and skills related to your egoic label can be a significant advantage in building a successful business. By leveraging your knowledge and expertise, you can create valuable content and products that resonate with your audience and set you apart from your competitors.

Question 4. Does this egoic label have a problem to solve?

The fourth question in the audience filter scorecard is, "Does this egoic label have a problem to solve?" This question is important because businesses that solve customer problems are more likely to be successful.

Warby Parker is one business that identified a problem and successfully solved it. Warby Parker is an eyewear company that was founded in 2010. The company's founders, Neil Blumenthal and Dave Gilboa, identified a problem in the eyewear industry: high prices for glasses.

Blumenthal and Gilboa noticed that the eyewear industry was dominated by a few large companies that charged high prices for glasses. They believed this pricing model was unfair to customers and set out to create an alternative.

Warby Parker's business model is based on offering affordable, stylish glasses to customers. The company designs and manufactures its own glasses, cutting out the middleman and reducing costs. This allows Warby Parker to offer glasses at a fraction of the cost of traditional eyewear companies.

Warby Parker's focus on solving a customer problem has helped it succeed tremendously. The company has grown rapidly and is now valued at over $3 billion. Its success shows that identifying a problem and finding a unique solution can be a recipe for success.[14]

In conclusion, businesses that solve problems for their customers are more likely to be successful. By identifying a problem and finding a unique solution, you can create a business that truly resonates with your audience and sets you apart from your competitors.

Question 5. Are other businesses earning money helping this egoic label?

The fifth question in the audience filter scorecard is, "Are other businesses earning money helping this egoic label?" This question is important because it can help you to determine whether there is a viable market for your business.

DAY 7. THE AUDIENCE FILTER SCORECARD

It's important to remember that competition is not necessarily a bad thing. In fact, the presence of other businesses successfully serving your target audience can be a good sign. It means there is a market for your business, and people are willing to pay for products and services related to your egoic label.

By researching other businesses in your field, you can learn from their successes and failures. You can identify what they are doing well and what you can do better. This can help you create a unique value proposition and differentiate yourself from competitors.

For example, let's say that you are passionate about fitness and want to create an online fitness coaching business. By researching other online fitness coaching businesses, you can identify what they are doing well and what you can do better. Perhaps you notice that other businesses are focused on weight loss, but there is a lack of content for people who want to gain muscle. By focusing on this niche, you can differentiate yourself from your competitors and create a unique value proposition for your audience.

In conclusion, researching other businesses in your field can be valuable when building your business. By identifying what is working and what can be improved, you can create a unique value proposition and differentiate yourself from your competitors. Remember, competition is not bad – it can be a sign of a viable market for your business.

Question 6. Do I want to serve this egoic label?

The final question in the audience filter scorecard is, "Do I want to serve this egoic label?" This question is essential because it determines whether you are motivated to serve your audience beyond just making a profit.

As a writer, coach, or course creator, your primary goal should be to serve your audience and help them achieve their goals. While making a profit is important for any business, it should not be the sole focus. Your passion for serving your audience and helping them succeed should be your business's driving force.

By focusing on serving your audience, you can create products and services that truly resonate with them. You can create a community of loyal followers who share your passion and vision. This can help you create a sustainable and fulfilling business that positively impacts people's lives.

For example, you are a writer passionate about personal development. Your goal should be to create content that helps your readers to grow and achieve their goals.

While earning a living from your writing is important, your primary focus should be serving your audience and helping them improve their lives.

In conclusion, as a writer, coach, or course creator, it's important to focus on serving your audience and helping them to achieve their goals.

Doing so can create a sustainable, fulfilling business that positively impacts people's lives. While profit-making is important, it should not be the sole focus. Your passion for serving your audience should be the driving force behind your business.

Time to Rate Yourself

Rate each question on a scale of one to ten, with ten being the highest score. The highest score you can get for each egoic label is 60 (10 for each question). Add the scores for each egoic label and write down the top three.

If you started with three egoic labels, pick your top one. It's important to decide on one to focus on moving forward.

Treat this process as a practice business if making decisions is tough for you. Approach it as if you were trading paper money in the stock market before using real money. Use this exercise to educate yourself and build your skills.

I want to help...	Egoic Label #1	Egoic Label #2	Egoic Label #3
1. Do I enjoy learning about this egoic label?	/10	/10	/10
2. Am I passionate about this egoic label?	/10	/10	/10
3. Do I have experience or skills related to this egoic label?	/10	/10	/10
4. Does this egoic label have a problem to solve?	/10	/10	/10
5. Are other businesses earning money helping this egoic label?	/10	/10	/10
6. Do I want to serve this egoic label?	/10	/10	/10
Total Score:	/60	/60	/60

Once you have selected your top egoic label, we can move on to the next day in the challenge.

You have taken a logical and practical approach to finding your dream customers by identifying your audience using the filter scorecard.

Keep in mind that it's important to choose an egoic label that you are passionate about and have experience or skills related to.

This will help you to create content and products that truly resonate with your audience.

Day 7 Exercise: Complete the Audience Filter Scorecard

Complete the Audience Filter Scorecard and narrow your audience to one egoic label.

Day 7 Key Takeaways:

- The audience filter scorecard is a useful tool for identifying your target audience.
- The scorecard helps you to approach audience identification in a logical, step-by-step manner.
- The first step is identifying your egoic label(s) and defining your identity and interests.
- The scorecard asks six questions about your egoic label(s), including whether you enjoy learning about them, whether you are passionate about them, and whether there is a problem to solve for that egoic label.
- Having experience and skills related to your egoic label is an advantage in building a successful business and helps to create valuable content and products.

- Researching other businesses in your field can help you to identify what is working and what can be improved upon and to create a unique value proposition.

- Passion is a powerful force that can drive business success and inspire others.

- While profit-making is important, it should not be the sole focus. The primary focus should be serving your audience and helping them achieve their goals.

- A successful business can be built by identifying a problem and finding a unique solution that resonates with your audience.

Overall, the audience filter scorecard is a powerful tool that can help you to create a sustainable and fulfilling business by identifying your target audience and their needs. By focusing on serving your audience and creating unique value, you can create a business that positively impacts people's lives.

8
Day 8. Discovering Your Audience's Goals

Emily was a young graphic designer who loved working on various design projects. But she wasn't making enough money to support herself. She knew she had to specialize in something to make a name for herself and earn a decent income. So, she started researching different design niches to find the one that was both in demand and aligned with her interests.

After much research and experimentation, Emily found her niche in book cover design. She discovered that many self-published authors needed quality book covers to attract potential readers. So, she focused her efforts on creating beautiful and professional book covers that would help authors stand out from the competition.

Emily's book cover designs were a hit, and soon she became the go-to person for self-published authors. She marketed her services on social media and built a strong online presence. Word of mouth soon spread, and her business grew exponentially.

As her business grew, Emily continued to refine her skills and adapt to the market's changing demands. She learned about the latest design trends and incorporated them into her work. She also diversified her services to include book cover design and formatting and editing services for self-published authors.

Today, Emily is a successful and sought-after book cover designer, and her business is thriving. She has expanded her services to include publishing and marketing, and she has a team of designers who work with her to meet the growing demand for her services.

Emily's story is an excellent example of how finding a profitable niche can help you grow your business and achieve your financial goals. By specializing in book cover design, Emily established herself as an expert in her field, attracted a loyal following, and built a thriving business.

Day 8. Discovering Your Audiences Goals

Over the next few days, we'll do a deep dive into your chosen egoic label. By the end, you'll know your audience in a deep and profound way. But how do you do that? Well, you will use something I created called the Audience GPS system. This system is like a guidance system, but it's an audience GPS, which stands for Goals, Passions, and Struggles.

Goals: Why Understanding Your Audience's Goals Is Critical to Your Business Success

Discovering what your ideal audience wants is crucial to building a successful business. Your audience's goals will help you determine what they are looking for and what they need, and this knowledge can help you create products or services that address those needs effectively.

Understanding the objectives of your audience is a key factor in creating a winning business. For example, if your audience's goal is to improve their fitness, your marketing messages can focus on the benefits of your fitness program, how it can help them achieve their health and fitness goals, and why it's the best option for them.

Also, understanding your audience's goals will help you create more engaging and relevant content. If your audience is interested in starting a business, for instance, you can create blog posts, podcasts, and videos that offer tips and advice on how to start a successful business.

In addition to these benefits, knowing your audience's goals can help you create better products or services. By understanding what your audience is looking for, you can effectively create a product or service that meets their needs. This can help you to build a devoted customer base and differentiate yourself from competitors.

It's important to note that your audience's goals can change over time, and keeping up with these changes is essential. You can do this by keeping track of trends, listening to customer feedback, and staying up to date with changes in your industry.

Knowing the goals of your audience is crucial for building a successful business. It can help you to tailor your marketing messages, create engaging content, and develop a suite of products that meet the needs of your audience effectively. By understanding your audience's goals, you can build a strong connection with them and position your business for long-term success.

Passions: How to Use Audience Passions to Build a Loyal Following for Your Business

Understanding your audience's passions is just as important as understanding their goals. When you know what your audience is passionate about, you can create content and products that resonate with them on a deeper level. This can help you to build a strong bond with your audience and increase their loyalty to your brand.

One example of a company that understands the importance of understanding its audience's passions is Patagonia. Patagonia has built its brand around a commitment to sustainability. This passion is reflected in their products, designed to help outdoor enthusiasts enjoy the outdoors while minimizing their environmental impact. Patagonia's commitment to these values has helped them to build a loyal following of customers who share these passions.

Studies have shown that understanding your audience's passions can significantly impact your marketing success. A study by the marketing research firm Mintel found that 70% of consumers are more likely to make a purchase from a brand that shares their values.[15] This highlights the importance of understanding your audience's passions and values in building a strong connection with them.

Understanding the passions of your audience is crucial for building a successful business. It can help you to create products and services that resonate with your audience on a deeper level and build a loyal following of customers who share your brand's values. By understanding your audience's passions, you can position your business for long-term success and differentiate yourself from competitors.

Struggles: How to Create Solutions That Address Your Audience's Struggles

Understanding the struggles of your egoic label is critical to building a successful online business. When you understand the problems that your audience is facing, you can create products or services that effectively address those issues. This can help you to build a devoted customer base and position your online business for long-term success.

In the early 20th century, Henry Ford recognized that many people were struggling to afford cars. He understood that if he could make cars more affordable, he could tap into a large and untapped market of potential customers.

Ford implemented a revolutionary production method known as the assembly line to address this issue. This method allowed Ford to produce cars more efficiently and at a lower cost, which allowed him to sell them at a lower price. This made cars more affordable for the average person, and it helped Ford to build a loyal customer base and position his business for long-term success.[16]

This example demonstrates the importance of understanding your audience's struggles and creating products or services that address those struggles effectively. By understanding the problems that your audience is facing, you can create solutions that meet their needs and provide them with real value. This can help you to differentiate yourself from competitors and build a strong brand that resonates with your audience.

Understanding your audience's struggles can also help you identify new opportunities for growth and innovation. By understanding the problems that your audience is facing, you can identify gaps in the market where you can fulfill your audience's needs. This helps you to stay ahead of the curve and positions your business for continued growth and success.

Start by Finding Your Audience's Goals

In future chapters, we will give you some specific exercises to uncover your audience's passions and struggles. Today, let's start by uncovering their goals.

In the digital age, connecting with your target audience has never been more accessible. One of the keys to successful online engagement is understanding your audience's goals and how they consume content. This helps you create relevant and valuable material and ensures that your message reaches them through their preferred medium. In this chapter, we will explore the importance of online research to uncover your audience's interests and identify which content format resonates with them most.

Identify Active Blogs in Your Niche

Exploring popular blogs within your niche will help you get a pulse on your audience's interests, concerns, and goals. By analyzing the most-read and shared content, you can identify trending topics and tailor your offerings to address these shared needs.

You can use search engines and social media platforms to find active niche blogs to explore keywords related to your industry. Also, visiting other experts' and influencers' websites can help you identify further inspiration and gather insights about the topics that resonate most with your audience.

Scout for Popular Podcasts

Podcasts are a fast-growing medium, with listeners seeking information, education, and entertainment on a variety of subjects. Investigating popular podcasts in your niche can provide valuable context on your audience's goals and preferences.

You can use podcast directories, apps, and platform-specific search tools to discover relevant podcasts. Explore the top-ranked episodes and take note of the themes, questions, and expert insights shared.

This will provide you with a better understanding of what your audience is interested in and how you can address it in your content.

I like to use ListenNotes.com to scout out if there are any popular podcasts in a niche.

Search for Trending YouTube Videos

Visual content is incredibly engaging, which is evident in the popularity of platforms like YouTube. Exploring video content within your niche will further unveil your audience members' trends, tastes, and goals.

To find videos related to your niche, use YouTube's search feature and filters, such as date, relevance, and view count. Analyzing the most-viewed and highly-rated videos will provide valuable information on what your audience is passionate about and seeking.

You can also use the advanced search to view just YouTube Channels in your niche. You want to see that there are popular YouTube Channels in your niche, especially if video is part of your content plan.

Uncovering Your Audience's Preferred Content Medium

While researching the various content channels—blogs, podcasts, and videos—pay attention to which medium appears most popular within your niche.

- Are there more active blogs than podcasts?
- Do the most active podcasts have lots of reviews?
- Do YouTube videos receive more engagement than written

DAY 8. DISCOVERING YOUR AUDIENCE'S GOALS

articles?

The answers will help you determine the most effective format for presenting your message and attracting your target audience.

Identifying your audience's preferred medium can significantly improve the success of your online business by creating the most engaging and relevant content. Knowing whether to focus on written, audio, or visual content will ensure your message and solutions reach your audience in a way that resonates with them best.

Understanding your audience's goals and interests is essential to building a successful online business. By conducting thorough research on blogs, podcasts, and YouTube videos, you can uncover valuable insights into your niche, helping you tailor your content to your target audience's preferences. These findings will also pinpoint which medium your niche tends to consume most, ensuring that you prioritize the most impactful format for your business and further foster connections with your audience.

Day 8 Exercise: Write Down Your Audience's Goals

Create a list of aspirational goals your ideal customer wants to accomplish based on the research you performed.

Day 8 Key Takeaways:

- Understanding your audience's goals is crucial for creating content and products that resonate with them and building a strong connection.

- Knowing your audience's passions helps you create products and services that resonate with them on a deeper level and build a loyal following.

- Understanding your audience's struggles is critical for creating solutions that meet their needs and provide real value, leading to a loyal customer base and long-term success.

- Historical examples like Henry Ford demonstrate the importance of understanding your audience's struggles and addressing them effectively.

- By understanding your audience's goals, passions, and struggles, you can identify new opportunities for growth and innovation, stay ahead of the curve, and position your business for continued success.

9
Day 9. Finding Your Audience's Passions

Imagine the early days of the Internet when people from all around the world started sharing their thoughts on what was yet to be known as "blogs." A specific platform designed to connect people with similar interests, passions, and struggles did not exist back then.

Today, however, we live in a world with countless blogging niches. But how can you find the one that resonates with your audience, and more importantly, how can you identify your target audience's passions?

Consider for a moment the story of a woman named Shelly, who had a strong passion for crafting and DIY projects. In search of an online community, she found a blog that shared step-by-step tutorials on how to create hand-made home decorations and hosted discussions on various craft materials and techniques.

Intrigued, Shelly became an avid reader of this blog and eventually started her own blog, sharing her creations with others who had similar passions. Had the creator of the initial blog not investigated and tapped into Shelly's passion for crafting, they may have never connected.

This chapter is designed to help you explore the passions of your potential audience by identifying if your chosen topic is something people genuinely care about and have consistently searched for over time. We will guide you through comparing your niche with others, spotting trends, and avoiding fads or evergreen niches.

We will also delve into methods for measuring enthusiasm and overall interest in your niche through platforms like LinkedIn and Facebook groups. By the end of this chapter, you will have the tools and knowledge necessary to pinpoint your audience's passions and build a successful, engaging blog around them.

Are you ready to embark on this journey and find out what truly sets your readers' hearts on fire?

Day 9. Finding Your Audiences Passions

Google Trends is a powerful resource for understanding your target audience's interests and ensuring that your chosen niche is consistent, particularly when you start a blog or create content around new ideas. For example, let's say you want to start a blog on gardening. You might be interested in exploring the level of interest and consistency in people's search patterns related to organic gardening or urban gardening. By utilizing Google Trends and setting the time frame to one year or even extending it to five years, you'll get valuable insights into the popularity of these gardening sub-niches.

Suppose you find out that urban gardening has shown a steady and consistent growth in search popularity over the past few years. This information can aid you in focusing your content on urban gardening, which is apparently a growing and sustainable interest among your audience. In contrast, if your initial idea for a niche showed a decline or was flat in search popularity, it may be worth reconsidering or pivoting to a more engaging topic.

Let's take another example: what if you want to launch a travel blog? With the popularity of experiences like van life, eco-travel, and digital nomad lifestyle, it might be hard to decide on which sub-niche to focus. By comparing the search consistency for each of these terms on Google Trends, you can determine which of these sub-niches has displayed a sustainable interest among readers over the past few years. If you find that eco-travel has been an area of consistent growth, then you can align your content creation with this trend, reaching more passionate readers and increasing your chances of building an engaged community.

Google Trends can also help you identify seasonal patterns in search volume for your niche. For instance, if you want to create content around winter sports, you can expect fluctuations in search popularity due to the seasonal nature of the topic. By using Google Trends, you can recognize these patterns and plan your content strategy accordingly, ensuring that your blog remains consistent and relevant to your audience throughout the year.

In summary, using Google Trends as a tool to measure consistency is an essential step in finding the right niche for your blog. It will empower you to make informed decisions, avoid fads or evergreen niches, and ensure you are addressing the passions and interests of your audience effectively. With a consistent and profitable niche, you are setting yourself up for greater chances of success in the world of blogging.

Identifying Trends Using Proven Niches

Using proven niches as a yardstick for evaluating the consistency of your proposed niche can save you time and increase your chances of success in your blogging endeavor. By analyzing the search volumes in your chosen field and comparing them to proven niches, you can identify promising niches and avoid highly competitive or saturated areas.

For instance, imagine you are passionate about health and fitness and are considering starting a blog on healthy meal planning. By comparing your idea with a few proven niches, such as yoga, running, and meditation, you can see if the search volumes align.

If the search volumes for your niche slightly overlap or are only a bit lower than those of the proven niches, you could score a yellow, indicating potential in your specific sub-niche without significantly high competition.

Another example might be if you wish to create content around personal finance. To measure the consistency of your chosen niche, you can compare it to proven niches like investing, budgeting, and retirement planning. If you find that their search volumes are in line with personal finance savings tips, for example, it could indicate a promising and consistent niche worthy of your time and effort.

On the other hand, if you have an interest in starting a fashion blog that focuses on a specific style, such as sustainable fashion, you can investigate the consistency of this niche by comparing it to proven areas like women's fashion, men's fashion, and clothing accessories. If the search volumes remain high or even trend upwards, you are likely onto a winning idea.

Recognizing trends through the comparison of your selected niche to proven niches can provide you with valuable insights into the potential profitability and sustainability of your blog idea. Not only will this technique help to predict the success of your chosen niche, but it will also prevent you from diving into overly competitive and saturated markets.

By identifying and selecting a consistent niche, you are placing yourself in an advantageous position for future growth and success in the blogging world.

Beware of Fads

Fads are temporary trends that often catch people's attention for a brief period, seemingly taking the world by storm, only to die out as quickly as they came. These short-lived crazes can be tempting to capitalize on, but doing so can ultimately lead you to short-lived success rather than a sustainable and profitable business in the long run. Consequently, it is essential to be cautious and avoid delving into fad niches when building a blog or business.

A prime example of a fad is the Pokémon Go phenomenon in 2016. At its peak, the augmented reality game captured the attention of millions of users worldwide. Businesses catering to the craze, from themed merchandise to restaurant promotions, sprang up overnight, only to see their traffic and revenues dwindle as the hype faded.

Another illustrative example is kale, which gained immense popularity as a superfood a few years ago. Restaurants and food bloggers alike tapped into the trend by creating kale-centric recipes, smoothies, and even chips. While kale's healthy properties still hold value, its brief fame has waned, and those who built their business solely on the "kale wagon" experienced a decline in interest.

The key to avoiding fads lies in thorough research and analysis of your target market. Investigate the history and longevity of your niche or sub-niche by looking at factors such as customer reviews, search volumes on Google Trends, and the presence of well-established businesses or blogs within your chosen field. If a topic has enjoyed steady interest and growth over several years, it is likely not a fad.

Ultimately, the success of your blog or business relies on focusing on topics that people have consistently found valuable, informative, and relevant over time. Although fads have their appeal and potential for short-term profits, they are not conducive to building a long-lasting and impactful legacy through your content.

By researching your niche and following the guidance offered in this chapter, you can confidently steer clear of fleeting trends and establish a sustainable business centered around your target audience's genuine passions and interests.

Measuring Enthusiasm Using LinkedIn and Facebook

Measuring enthusiasm among your target audience is an essential factor in ensuring the sustainability and success of your blog or business. LinkedIn and Facebook, two social networking giants, can provide valuable insights into the level of enthusiasm for your selected niche.

In the case of LinkedIn, consider searching for your niche or sub-niche and exploring the number of available groups. For example, if you plan to start a blog on vegan cooking, look up vegan-related groups on LinkedIn. If you find numerous groups with several active members, it reflects a keen interest in your topics. The same goes for other sub-niches such as plant-based diets or gluten-free cooking - if there are several active groups present, it speaks to a passionate audience.

Facebook groups serve as another excellent resource for gauging enthusiasm. To make the most of this method, search for groups related to your niche and assess the frequency of posts and interactions within these communities. Returning to our vegan cooking example, search for Facebook groups such as "Vegan Recipes" or "Vegan Cooking 101." Pay attention to daily posts and lively discussions, which indicate a genuinely engaged and enthusiastic audience.

DAY 9. FINDING YOUR AUDIENCE'S PASSIONS

For example, you might come across a vegan recipe group with hundreds of daily posts, numerous members sharing feedback, asking questions, and demonstrating a genuine interest in learning and exploring plant-based cooking. Such a group would testify to a robust and passionate audience in your chosen niche.

Besides understanding audience enthusiasm, these platforms also offer potential collaborations and networking opportunities. As you build your blog or business, connecting with like-minded individuals from your niche or joining relevant conversations can help you establish your presence and further validate the passions of your target audience.

By leveraging social networking platforms like LinkedIn and Facebook groups, you gain not only access to a treasure trove of authentic audience enthusiasm indicators but also a channel to network with like-minded individuals nurturing a growing community around your niche. Armed with these insights, you can create content that resonates deeply with your audience, solidifying your position as an expert within your area of passion.

Finding the right niche for your blog is key to building an engaged community of readers. This chapter has provided essential tips for identifying and measuring passion and consistency in your chosen niche, avoiding fads, and leveraging social networking platforms to assess audience enthusiasm and network with fellow bloggers or businesses.

You can ensure consistency and potential profitability by using Google Trends to evaluate your niche's search popularity and comparing it to proven niches. At the same time, social networking platforms like LinkedIn and Facebook groups can offer valuable insights into the level of enthusiasm for your chosen sub-niche. Remember to be thorough in your research to avoid fads and stay focused on passions that people have consistently found valuable, informative, and relevant over time.

Day 9 Exercise: Measure Your Audience's Passion (and Enthusiasm)

- Go to Google Trends and search for your niche or sub-niche. Set the timeframe to the past year or five years.

- Compare your search results to those of established or popular niches to determine consistency and potential profitability.

- Explore LinkedIn and Facebook groups related to your niche, paying attention to the frequency and enthusiasm of posts and discussions.

Day 9 Key Takeaways:

- Google Trends is a powerful tool for measuring consistency and potential profitability in your chosen niche.

- Comparing your search results to proven niches can help you determine the consistency of your chosen sub-niche - and whether it's worthy of investing time and effort.

- Beware of fads - focus on passions that have proven sustainability rather than short-lived crazes.

- Social networking platforms like LinkedIn and Facebook groups offer invaluable insights into audience enthusiasm and networking opportunities.

10

Day 10. Uncovering Your Audience's Struggles

Do you know that the e-learning industry is expected to be worth $325 billion by 2025?[17] This mind-blowing statistic demonstrates the limitless opportunities that exist for those eager to monetize their passion and expertise by exploring various income streams. Are you ready to unlock the full potential of your niche by capitalizing on this vast market?

In this chapter, I'll reveal the secrets to creating a successful blog or online business by combining four primary income streams: Writer, Coach, Teacher, and Speaker. Unleash the power of Amazon, Clarity.fm, Udemy.com, and Google in your quest to find engaging and profitable topics within your niche. With specific examples and step-by-step guidance, you'll learn how to validate the demand for your products and services, ensuring your audience is willing to pay before you create the offerings they crave.

Don't miss your chance to become a master of income diversification as you grow your online presence and solidify your reputation as a go-to expert in your niche. Ready to embark on this thrilling journey? Let's dive in!

Day 10. Uncovering Your Audience's Struggles

As we continue on our journey to build a successful blog or online business, it's crucial to understand the various income streams that can come from your chosen niche. In this chapter, I will explore four primary income streams: Writer, Coach, Teacher, and Speaker. For each income stream, I'll provide specific examples and illustrations to give you a clearer picture of how to monetize your passion.

Writer Income Streams: The Importance of Identifying Profitable Topics on Amazon

Before delving into creating valuable content for your niche, it's essential to confirm that your audience is willing to pay for the information you are going to provide. As one of the largest online marketplaces, Amazon is an excellent starting point to determine the demand for eBooks, print books, and audiobooks related to your niche. By analyzing Amazon's customer behavior and trends, you can ensure that people are paying money to solve specific problems before you create products to address their needs.

Digital Books

The digital revolution has made eBooks a popular and cost-effective means of sharing knowledge with a vast audience. Amazon's Kindle Direct Publishing (KDP) enables you to self-publish your eBook and reach millions of readers worldwide.

To validate the potential for success in your chosen niche, analyze the number of reviews and sponsored ads related to the topic on Amazon.

For instance, if self-improvement is your niche, you might observe numerous eBooks on topics like time management or productivity, showcasing a strong demand for such content.

Print Books

Although eBooks are gaining popularity, print books still generate substantial income for writers who invest time in crafting well-researched and engaging content. Platforms like Amazon's CreateSpace or IngramSpark provide wide distribution, allowing you to reach target audiences through various channels. To assess the demand and potential profitability for print books in your niche, analyze Amazon customer reviews and sales rankings of top-selling books.

For example, let's say you specialize in health and wellness. By researching top-selling books on Amazon, you can identify specific sub-topics with high demand, such as plant-based diets or mindfulness meditation. This insight will give you a better understanding of which topics to focus on when creating your print book.

Audiobooks

Audiobooks are a rapidly growing segment in the publishing industry, with more and more people opting for this convenient format to consume content. Amazon's Audible platform offers a vast selection of audiobooks in various niches. Similar to eBooks and print books, validating the demand for audiobooks in your niche is crucial before diving into production.

Analyze the reviews, sales rankings, and customer ratings of audiobooks related to your niche on Audible. For example, if your focus is personal finance, you might observe high ratings and numerous reviews for audiobooks on topics such as investing, budgeting, or retirement planning, revealing strong demand and potential for success in this niche.

Researching Amazon customer trends for eBooks, print books, and audiobooks is crucial in determining the demand and potential profitability of your chosen niche. By analyzing reviews, sales rankings, and ratings, you can confidently create products that cater to your audience's needs and capitalize on the income opportunities within your niche.

Coaching Income Streams: Using Clarity.fm to Find Coaching Trends

If you're exploring ways to monetize your online business, offering coaching services is a profitable route to take. However, before creating coaching packages, it's essential to ensure if your audience is willing to pay for coaching services within your niche. Clarity.fm helps to simplify this process by revealing the topics in your niche that your audience is paying for coaching. Let's look at how we can use Clarity.fm to do market research for our coaching practice.

Search for Your Niche

Begin your search on Clarity.fm by entering your niche topic and browsing through coaches' profiles. Look for coaches with numerous reviews, high ratings, and positive comments. Ideally, you want to discover coaches who are solving problems similar to the ones you can solve for your audience.

Examples of Popular Niche Topics

When searching for coaches in popular niches like blogging and stock investing, you can quickly identify multiple coaches with excellent ratings and reviews. This validates that people are willing to pay for expert guidance, making coaching an ideal income stream opportunity for your online business.

In summary, Clarity.fm provides valuable insights into the earning potential of coaching services within your niche. Using this platform, you can identify what topics your audience is willing to pay for, helping to create targeted coaching programs that align with your audience's needs.

Teacher Income Streams: Discover Coaching Trends Through Market Research

Being a subject matter expert on a topic puts you in a great position to create and sell online courses and memberships. However, before diving into content creation, it's crucial to conduct market research and validate the demand for specific pain points that your audience is willing to pay for. One such platform that can give you invaluable insights into this is Udemy.com.

Search for Your Niche on Udemy.com

Begin your market research by searching for courses related to your niche on Udemy.com. Keep an eye on factors like the number of reviews, ratings, and overall student engagement with the course material. These indicators can help to assess the demand for particular topics within your niche.

Examples of Finding Opportunities

For instance, consider the topic of kettlebell fitness. On Udemy, you might come across courses with fewer reviews than you had anticipated. While it may not be perfect from the get-go, it showcases a potential income stream.

This indicates that there's an opportunity for you to create an insightful and engaging course about kettlebell fitness, helping others while establishing a reliable teacher income stream. Finding successful courses with lots of reviews is a good thing. It means your audience wants to pay for and consume online courses to help them achieve their desired goals. In conclusion, Udemy.com is a valuable resource for discovering opportunities within your niche for creating online courses and memberships. By understanding the demand, you can focus on the topics that your audience is willing to pay for, ensuring the success of your online business.

Speaker Income Streams: Unlock Speaking Gigs Through Google Searches

Do you love speaking and sharing your wisdom with others? Embarking on a journey as a speaker can open up new income streams through conferences, workshops, and events. To determine the potential in your niche, you can rely on Google to find speaking opportunities that showcase your expertise.

Discover Your Niche Conferences and Events

To kick-start your search for speaking engagements, use Google to explore conferences, workshops, or associations closely related to your niche.

The primary objective is to pinpoint events where your distinct knowledge and expertise can provide genuine value to the attendees, bolstering your reputation as a go-to speaker in your field.

Identify the Right Keywords

Make use of specific and relevant keywords while browsing for events that match your niche. Consider the terms and phrases your target audience will most likely use when looking for content within your expertise.

Choosing optimal keywords will improve the quality of your search results, making it easier to find niche-targeted conferences and events. For example, in addition to your niche keyword also insert words like conference, event, or workshop.

Monitor Event Calendars

Keep an eye on event calendars and listings within your niche. Many industry associations and websites provide event calendars for members and visitors, which can offer a wealth of information regarding upcoming conferences and workshops. Regularly check these listings to stay informed and remain up-to-date with potential speaking opportunities.

Connect with Industry Influencers

Establishing connections within your niche can enhance your chances of discovering speaking opportunities. Reach out to industry influencers, engage with their content, and join online communities to network with like-minded professionals. Forming these alliances can lead to collaboration, referrals, and invitations to speak at prominent events.

By conducting well-targeted searches and actively engaging with your niche community, you can identify events where your skills can provide immense value and contribute to your growth as a go-to speaker. Networking and staying informed are crucial to uncovering and capitalizing on speaker income streams within your niche.

Examples of Speaker Opportunities

Let's take business travel as an example. When searching for events and conferences related to business travel, you might come across different gatherings where speakers are presenting their expertise and insights on productivity and tips related to business travel.

This illustrates that there's a demand for subject matter experts in the niche. Consequently, you have the opportunity to tap into this market and create another income stream as a speaker.

In summary, using Google to find conferences and events in your niche can uncover numerous opportunities to engage with your audience and establish yourself as a speaker.

Capitalize on these opportunities to share your expertise and diversify your income streams effectively.

Now, it's your turn.

As we conclude this insightful chapter, it's essential to remember that developing a successful blog or online business involves tapping into various income streams.

By leveraging your expertise as a Writer, Coach, Teacher, and Speaker, you can build a profitable and fulfilling business that addresses your audience's needs and resonates with their passions.

You now know how utilizing tools like Amazon, Clarity.fm, Udemy.com, and Google can help you find and validate the demand for your niche offerings.

It's time to put that knowledge to work and create income streams that support your goals, allowing you to turn your passion into a lucrative career.

Day 10 Exercise: Action Steps for Your Income Streams

1. Head over to Amazon, search for eBooks, print books, and audiobooks related to your niche, and analyze customer behavior by examining reviews and sales rankings.

2. Browse Clarity.fm to find coaches within your niche, looking for reviews, ratings, and engagement and determining if their offerings align with yours.

3. Research courses on Udemy.com related to your niche, examining factors like reviews, ratings, and student engagement.

4. Use Google to search for conferences, workshops, or associations relevant to your niche, and take note of the speaking opportunities that catch your attention.

Day 10 Key Takeaways:

- Utilize Amazon to explore the demand for eBooks, print books, and audiobooks in your niche, informing your decision on which products to create.

- Confirm the demand for coaching services within your niche by leveraging Clarity.fm, ensuring that your audience is willing to pay for your guidance.

- Use Udemy.com to examine the potential for creating online courses and memberships that cater to your audience's preferred topics.

- Search Google to unlock speaking opportunities by searching for niche conferences and events where you can share your expertise and build your reputation.

11

Day 11. How Will I Attract Them?

Imagine a world where your powerful message has the ability to inspire, motivate, and enlighten countless individuals, all eager to engage with your content. George Bernard Shaw once said, "The single biggest problem in communication is the illusion that it has taken place."[18] This leaves us with the important question: how do we successfully communicate in today's digitally-driven world?

In this chapter, we'll uncover the answer by exploring three remarkable platforms - blogging, podcasting, and YouTube - that provide an incredible opportunity to share your message, attract an engaged audience, and impact the lives of many.

Through real-life examples, industry tips, and step-by-step guidance, you'll gain the knowledge and insight to choose the perfect platform for your message and audience.

Day 11. Awareness: How Will I Attract Them?

By the end of this chapter, you'll be equipped with the necessary tools to take the first step toward building a loyal following, expanding your reach, and truly connecting with those who genuinely resonate with your message. The journey to share your message has never been more thrilling or essential - let's get started!

Blogging: Writing Your Way to Your Audience

As an influencer with a passion for writing, starting a blog is an ideal and natural choice. It allows you to connect with your audience, share your thoughts and experiences, and establish your expertise in your chosen niche. Here are several compelling reasons why starting a blog can be the perfect outlet for a writer influencer:

Authentic Expression of Your Thoughts

As a writer, you can uniquely express your thoughts and ideas with clarity and depth. A blog provides you the space to explore various topics, offer insights, and effectively communicate your perspective. It allows you to convey your thoughts with precision, making it much easier for your audience to understand and resonate with your message.

Building a Loyal Community

Writing has always been a powerful medium to connect with people who share your passions and values. By creating a blog, you can foster genuine connections with your readers through your writing style, subject matter, and storytelling abilities. Over time, these connections can evolve into a supportive and loyal community of readers who share your interests and eagerly await your next blog post.

Establishing Your Expertise

As a writer, you can use your blog to showcase your knowledge and skills in your chosen niche. Consistently sharing valuable and well-researched content will position you as a thought leader in your field, increasing your credibility and reach. Your blog can serve as a portfolio, showcasing your expertise and making it easier for potential clients or collaborators to discover and connect with you.

Opportunities for Monetization and Growth

A successful blog can open up numerous avenues for monetization and growth. From sponsored posts and affiliate marketing to digital products and online courses, a popular blog presents many ways to generate income. As your blog grows, you may be presented with new opportunities, such as speaking engagements, collaborations, or even book deals.

Flexibility and Creativity

A blog offers you the freedom to experiment with your writing and try unique ways of presenting your content. As a writer, this creative flexibility is invaluable as it allows you to continuously hone your voice and style. You can write about various subjects, share personal stories, or even invite guest bloggers to share their perspectives on your platform.

Blogging Statistics

Blogging is still a popular and effective way of reaching your audience. Here are some important statistics (Content Marketing Institute) that showcase the power of blogging:

- Websites with active blogs have 434% more indexed pages, which greatly improves search engine visibility.

- On average, companies that blog receive 97% more inbound links, increasing website traffic and potential for new readers.

- 82% of marketers who blog daily acquired a customer using their blog, versus only 57% of those who blog monthly.[2]

In conclusion, starting a blog is wise for influencers who find expression through writing. It allows you to share your thoughts and connect with others and presents opportunities for growth, monetization, and furthering your writing career. The power of the written word is immense, and by embracing your writing voice as an influencer, you have the potential to make a lasting impact on your audience.

Podcasting: Engaging Your Audience with Your Voice

As a coaching influencer, your strength lies in asking thought-provoking questions and guiding others towards personal growth and self-improvement. Starting a podcast is the perfect platform for someone with these skills, as it enables you to showcase your expertise and connect with your audience more intimately and personally.

Here are some key reasons to consider starting a podcast if your influencer voice is that of a coach:

Engaging Conversations and Deeper Insights

A podcast creates opportunities for stimulating conversations with interesting guests and inspiring figures in your niche. You can ask probing questions that yield deeper insights through interviews and discussions, helping your audience unravel complex concepts and make meaningful connections.

Your listeners will feel more included and engaged, as though they're part of the conversation, which will strengthen their connection to you and your coaching expertise.

Building Trust with Your Audience

The power of your voice, tone, and expression creates an authentic and intimate connection with your podcast listeners. As a coach, establishing trust is essential, and podcasting allows you to build this trust more effectively than written content. When your audience hears your voice and listens to how you navigate meaningful conversations, they'll develop a strong confidence in your abilities as a coach.

Showcasing Your Coaching Skills

A podcast is ideal for demonstrating your coaching skills, offering real-time discussions that showcase your ability to listen, empathize, and empower others.

Through live coaching sessions, Q&A episodes, and dialogues with industry experts, your podcast can be an invaluable tool for potential clients to experience your unique coaching approach and understand the transformational impact it can have on their lives.

Expanding Your Reach and Network

Starting a podcast helps you connect with other professionals and expand your network. By collaborating with thought leaders, fellow coaches, or influential guests, you'll gain access to their insights and experiences and extend your reach to their audiences.

This will help you grow your podcast community and provide opportunities for further collaboration, referrals, and enhancing your credibility as a coaching influencer.

On-Demand and Accessible Content

One significant advantage of podcasts is their on-demand and accessible nature. Time-poor individuals can listen to your podcast during commutes, workouts, or everyday tasks, making it easy for them to consume your content and put your coaching advice into practice.

The more accessible your content, the greater opportunity you have to impact your audience's lives and inspire them to grow. Podcasting is one of the most flexible forms of media as it does not require people to look at a screen like blogging and YouTube videos do.

Podcasting Statistics: Why it Matters

Podcasting has emerged as a popular and easy-to-consume form of content. Here are some compelling statistics (Edison Research) that illustrate the powerful impact of podcasting:

- 75% of Americans are familiar with the term "podcasting," and 50% have listened to a podcast.

- 37% of Americans have listened to a podcast in the last month, and around 24% have listened to one in the past week.

- Podcast listeners, on average, subscribe to seven different shows and listen to more than six hours of podcasts every week.[3]

As a coaching influencer who thrives on asking good questions, starting a podcast is a highly effective way to reach out to and engage with your audience. It allows you to build trust, showcase your expertise, grow your network, and share valuable, accessible content, making a podcast an excellent choice for those whose voice serves as a catalyst for personal growth and self-development.

YouTube: Making a Connection with Video

As an influencer with a knack for teaching or public speaking, starting a YouTube channel is a highly effective way to showcase your skills and connect with a global audience. YouTube's visual and interactive nature creates a dynamic learning environment for your viewers, making it an ideal platform for educators and speakers. Here are several compelling reasons why you should consider starting a YouTube channel if your influencer voice is that of a teacher or speaker:

Engaging and Interactive Learning Experience

You can transform your teaching or speaking skills with YouTube into visually engaging and interactive content. Demonstrations, tutorials, or TED-style talks will grab your audience's attention and help them better understand complex ideas while holding their interest. Moreover, YouTube allows you to utilize visual aids, such as graphics, slideshows, and animations, to further enhance your explanations, making your content both entertaining and educational.

Wider Audience and Greater Impact

Creating a YouTube channel allows you to reach a vast, global audience interested in learning new skills or seeking inspiration from thought-provoking speakers. Your videos can be accessed anytime and anywhere, allowing your viewers to learn at their own pace. As a result, your teachings and messages can have a broader impact, as you'll be reaching people far beyond your local community or immediate network.

Showcase of Expertise and Authority

Featuring your work on YouTube serves as a visual portfolio, showcasing your expertise and knowledge in your field. This increased visibility can enhance your credibility, attract new followers, and position yourself as a thought leader or an authority in your niche. Additionally, a well-maintained YouTube channel with engaging and educational content can open doors for new professional opportunities, such as speaking engagements, collaborations, and even book deals.

Strengthening the Personal Connection with Your Audience

The combination of your voice and on-screen presence can create a more personal connection with your viewers. This connection is crucial for nurturing trust, loyalty, and credibility as a teacher or speaker. By sharing relatable personal stories, anecdotes, or experiences, you allow your viewers to see the authentic and vulnerable side of you, further humanizing your teachings and creating an emotional bond with your audience.

Opportunity for Monetization and Growth

A successful YouTube channel offers various avenues for monetization and growth. There are numerous ways to generate revenue and expand your influence beyond your channel, from sponsored content, affiliate marketing, and display advertising to online courses and paid consultations.

As your YouTube presence grows, you'll see increased opportunities for collaborations, sponsorships, and partnerships with other brands and individuals within your industry. Let's take a closer look at the most recent YouTube statistics.

YouTube Statistics: Why it Matters

YouTube has experienced tremendous growth and has become a central hub for video content consumption. Here are some revealing statistics (YouTube) that demonstrate the powerful reach of this platform:

- YouTube has over 2 billion monthly logged-in users who watch videos.

- Users watch over a billion hours of video on YouTube every day.

- 70% of all YouTube watch time is generated by the platform's recommendation algorithm, which matches user interests with relevant content.[4]

By focusing on the "why" rather than just the "how," you'll be able to create content that truly resonates with your audience. This will help build trust and loyalty among your viewers and allow your YouTube channel to effectively reach the people who matter most to you. As you begin your YouTube journey, remember your purpose, vision, and ideal viewers. Embracing the "why" is essential to showcasing your way to your audience.

Starting a YouTube channel is an excellent choice for influencers with teaching or public speaking skills. The platform allows you to create visually engaging content, reach a wide audience, and establish your expertise while fostering strong emotional connections with your viewers. By leveraging your unique teaching or speaking talents, you have the potential to make a lasting and meaningful impact on the lives of your subscribers.

Now, it's your turn.

Throughout this chapter, we have explored the power and potential of blogging, podcasting, and YouTube as platforms to share your message and build awareness. Each platform offers unique advantages, and your choice depends on various factors, including your own preferences and the specific demands of your audience.

Day 11 Exercise: How Will You Attract Your Audience?

As we close this chapter, your Day 11 exercise is choosing whether to launch a blog, podcast, or YouTube channel. But what if you want to choose more than just one? For now, select the one content channel that best aligns with your influencer voice. You can always expand your reach later by launching one of the other two.

Day 11 Key Takeaways:

- Building awareness is essential for sharing your message, and choosing the right platform can greatly impact your success.

- Blogging is a timeless and powerful platform to share your message through writing, with a focus on consistency, quality, and promotion.

- Podcasting provides an intimate connection by allowing your audiences to engage with your voice, offering unique insights, and becoming a respected voice in your niche.

- YouTube delivers a rich, engaging experience by combining visual, auditory, and emotional elements, creating a memorable connection with your viewers.

- Regardless of the platform you choose, prioritize creating valuable content, engaging with your audience, and adopting effective promotion strategies for maximum impact.

Armed with the information and insights provided in this chapter, you are one step closer to selecting the ideal platform for sharing your message, attracting your target audience, and making a substantial impact on the lives of those who resonate with your message. Always remember, your message matters, and it's time to start sharing it with the world!

12

Day 12. How Will I Capture Them?

Did you know that for every $1 spent on email marketing, the average return on investment (ROI) is $42?[22] It's no wonder that having a strong email list has become an essential marketing tool for authors, coaches, speakers, bloggers, YouTubers, and podcasters alike. Strengthening and maintaining an engaged email list allows you to build lasting connections with your audience and can have a powerful impact on the success of your craft. This chapter focuses on capturing your audience's attention by building a thriving email list.

In an increasingly crowded digital world, creating genuine connections beyond the surface level is essential. Your email list is the key to nurturing these relationships and opening the door for increased opportunities for your career. By leveraging your writing, speaking, video, and podcasting skills with a dedicated, engaged email list, you can tap into a world of limitless potential for growth and success in your field.

In this chapter, we'll discuss the advantages of having an email list and share practical strategies for building it across various platforms. By implementing these tactics, you'll be well on your way to fostering deeper, more meaningful connections with your audience and setting the stage for long-lasting success. So, without further ado, let's dive into the world of email marketing and uncover the secrets to crafting an engaged, loyal, and ever-growing email list.

Day 12. Engagement: How Will I Capture Them?

An email list is one of the most effective ways to engage with your audience and have a consistent line of communication. Email allows you to reach your audience on a personal level, ensuring that your message gets across and stays relevant. Here are five big reasons why you should have an email list.

Reason 1. Personal Connection

Building an email list allows you to connect with your audience on a deeper level than social media or other online channels. When someone provides their email address, it's an invitation for you to communicate with them directly in their inbox, where they're most likely to see and, hopefully, read your message.

As an author, coach, or speaker, having a direct line of communication with your audience allows you to nurture relationships and create a meaningful impact on their lives.

Reason 2. Control Over Your Message

Social media platforms can be unpredictable. Algorithms change, and platforms adjust their features, making it increasingly challenging to remain visible and active. With an email list, you have the ultimate control over the message you want to share with your audience.

Your email content reaches your subscribers without being filtered or compromised by external factors that can affect your online presence. This control over your message is crucial when promoting books, courses, speaking events, or other products and services.

Reason 3. Increase Sales and Boost Revenue

An engaged email list is an invaluable resource when it comes to driving sales. By communicating directly with your audience, you can create strong and loyal connections, which often lead to a higher likelihood of your subscribers purchasing your books, coaching services, or attending your speaking events.

Research shows that email marketing can have an impressive return on investment (ROI) when executed correctly, making it an essential tool for those looking to grow their businesses.

Reason 4. Strengthen Credibility

An email list signifies a group of people who have voluntarily shown interest in your message and want to hear more from you. By consistently sending valuable and informative content, you can effectively establish yourself as an authority in your niche.

The more credibility you have as an author, coach, or speaker, the more referrals and new opportunities will come your way. An engaged email list can lead to more speaking engagements, coaching clients, and book sales.

Reason 5. Build a Community

One of the most rewarding aspects of an email list is the opportunity to build a community. An email list allows you to create a circle of dedicated fans and supporters who are genuinely interested in your message. You are fostering authentic connections with your audience by sharing your story and experiences with your subscribers and providing regular updates about your work. This sense of community creates loyalty to you and your work, leading to long-lasting relationships that will continuously support your career as an author, coach, or speaker.

Building an email list is vital to developing a successful career as an author, coach, or speaker. Maintaining direct connections with your audience allows you to readily share your message, build credibility, grow sales, and foster a supportive community. Now is the perfect time to start if you're not cultivating an email list.

Building an Email List with Blogging

The best way to build an email list with blogging primarily involves creating and sharing valuable content that caters to your target audience's interests while simultaneously offering them a reason to subscribe. Begin by consistently producing high-quality, informative, and engaging blog posts that address your readers' pain points or provide solutions to their challenges. By positioning yourself as a resource, you will establish trust and credibility with your audience, making them more inclined to sign up for your email list.

To entice readers to subscribe, create a lead magnet, such as a free ebook, checklist, or resource guide, that offers valuable insights or actionable items relevant to your niche. This lead magnet should be visually appealing, practical, and genuinely useful for your readers in order to reflect your expertise and the quality of content they can expect when joining your email list. Ensure your opt-in forms are strategically placed throughout your blog, on your sidebar, within relevant blog posts, or as a pop-up on your site, making it effortless for readers to sign up.

Additionally, promote your lead magnets and blog posts on social media to expand your reach, and collaborate with other bloggers or influencers in your niche to create guest posts. This generates opportunities for new audiences to discover your blog and encourages more sign-ups for your email list. By consistently delivering exceptional content, building credibility, and offering valuable incentives for joining your email list, you can effectively grow your subscriber base and create a loyal following through blogging.

Building an Email List with Podcasting

When it comes to building an email list with podcasting, it's crucial to leverage the power of your audio content and engage with your listeners effectively to motivate them to subscribe. To achieve this, ensure that your podcast episodes consistently deliver value, share actionable takeaways, and provide compelling insights that cater to your audience's interests. This creates trust and credibility among your listeners and keeps them coming back for more, increasing the likelihood of them signing up for your email list.

A convincing call-to-action (CTA) is essential for turning podcast listeners into email subscribers. Within each episode, mention a related resource or bonus content that listeners can access by signing up for your email list. This could include exclusive interviews, additional tips, and advice, or downloadable resources, such as guides or templates related to your industry. Make the process of signing up as seamless as possible by providing a short and memorable URL that directs listeners to a simple, aesthetically pleasing opt-in form. Repeat the CTA at the end of each episode to reinforce its importance and continuously drive listeners to sign up.

To further expand your reach and attract new subscribers, collaborate with other podcasters, industry experts, or influencers for interviews or guest appearances. These collaborations allow you to tap into their audience and bolster credibility, prompting more listeners to subscribe to your email list. You can effectively build an engaged email list that fosters strong connections with your audience by consistently offering valuable podcast content, including persuasive calls-to-action, and collaborating within your industry.

Building an Email List with YouTube

Building an email list with a YouTube channel involves creating high-quality, engaging video content that resonates with your target audience while encouraging them to subscribe for additional exclusive material. To captivate viewers and gain their trust, invest time and effort into producing visually appealing, informative, and valuable videos that address the questions and challenges faced by your audience. Establishing credibility and forming strong connections with your viewers will make them more inclined to join your email list.

Incorporate persuasive calls-to-action (CTAs) within your videos by briefly mentioning the benefits of signing up for your email list, such as access to exclusive content, subscriber-only discounts, or helpful resources. Utilize YouTube's annotations or interactive cards to create visually appealing, clickable links that direct viewers to a user-friendly, mobile-responsive signup form. Be transparent and straightforward about what your viewers will receive upon subscribing, and consistently reinforce these benefits throughout your videos to remind your audience of the value they will gain by joining your email list.

To further expand your reach and attract new subscribers, collaborate with other YouTube creators or influencers in your niche to create videos catering to your audiences. Also, implement YouTube SEO best practices, such as keyword-optimized titles, descriptions, and tags, to boost your channel's visibility and attract a broader audience. By coupling engaging video content with strategic calls-to-action and cross-promotion, you can build a thriving email list and foster a loyal viewership for your YouTube channel.

Building a strong email list is crucial for long-term success in fields such as authorship, coaching, speaking, blogging, podcasting, and video creation. By capturing your audience, you can establish stronger connections, build credibility, control your message, boost sales, and grow an engaged community that genuinely supports you. Whichever platform you choose, always focus on providing valuable content and incorporating compelling calls-to-action to persuade your audience to subscribe. Actively engage with your subscribers, nurture their trust, and utilize cross-promotion and collaborations to reach new followers and continue growing your email list.

Day 12 Exercise: Come Up with Your Lead Magnet

Brainstorm a list of two or three potential lead magnet ideas, such as eBooks, guides, checklists, or exclusive video content that would appeal to your target audience.

Day 12 Key Takeaways:

- Email lists allow you to communicate directly with your audience, maintaining control of your message and fostering personal connections.
- Building an email list boosts sales and strengthens your credibility as an author, coach, or speaker.
- Utilize lead magnets and strategic calls-to-action to encourage sign-ups across different platforms.
- Regularly produce valuable content that resonates with your audience and continually promotes your email list.

- Embrace collaborations with others in your niche to expand your reach and attract new subscribers.

13
Day 13. How Will I Help Them?

Did you know that 50% of all startups fail within the first four years, according to a recent report by Investopedia?[23] One of the primary reasons for this daunting statistic is entrepreneurs not validating their business ideas before venturing into the market. In today's fast-paced world, it is crucial not just to dream big but to build a solid foundation by testing your idea with real-life customers. So, how can we minimize the risk of failure and increase the chances of success in our endeavors? The answer lies in choosing the right validation offer.

In this chapter, we'll explore the concept of validation offers and dive deep into four different types of low-tech, easy-to-create products or services that can help you test the waters and find your footing in the market. By sharing an example from author and entrepreneur Pat Flynn, who validated his online course idea by pre-selling it to his audience before filming a single lesson, we'll show you that starting small and seeking feedback can help build trust, credibility, and a loyal following while building your dream business.

Let's embark on this exciting journey together and discover how choosing the right validation offer can transform your passion and message into a thriving and sustainable endeavor. Success awaits those who do their due diligence before taking the plunge!

Day 13. Conversion: How Will I Help Them?

Welcome to Day 13! Today is all about serving your audience in a way that aligns with your passion and message. This means picking a validation offer. A validation offer is a low-tech, simple product or service that allows you to test the waters in your market. You'll see if people truly want it before investing lots of time or money.

In this chapter, we'll discuss four different validation offers. Choose the one that best matches your skills and expertise—writing a short Kindle book, launching a 4-week bootcamp, creating a mini-course, or hosting a 1-day virtual workshop.

What is a Validation Offer?

A validation offer is a crucial step in the process of building your business, as it allows you to test the waters and determine if there is genuine interest for your product or service before fully diving in.

Think of it as a way to "dip your toes" in the market, gathering valuable insights, feedback, and gauging the true demand for what you have to offer. By starting small with a low-tech and easy-to-create product or service, you minimize the upfront investment and quickly identify if your idea has potential.

The importance of a validation offer cannot be overstated. It not only helps in reducing the time, effort, and money spent on developing a more extensive offering, but it also helps you fine-tune your messaging and understand your target audience better. With a validation offer, you can quickly adapt and adjust your strategy based on the feedback you receive, which is invaluable for making data-driven decisions and enhancing your overall marketing efforts.

A validation offer serves as a stepping stone for building trust and credibility with your audience. By delivering a high-quality product or service that resonates with your target customers, you establish yourself as an authority in your niche and create a loyal following. This connection with your audience will benefit you tremendously as you expand your business and release more advanced offers in the future.

In conclusion, a validation offer is essential for testing the market and understanding the true potential of your idea. It saves you time, resources, and lays a solid foundation for your business, making it an indispensable tool for any budding entrepreneur or content creator looking to make a meaningful impact on their target audience.

Validate Offer 1. Write a Short Kindle Book (Writer Influencer)

Are you a writer? Then consider writing a short Kindle book as your validation offer.

Writing a short Kindle book is the perfect starting point for writers looking to establish themselves in today's digital landscape. It offers various benefits and opportunities, making it an excellent option for writers entering the world of self-publishing.

Writing a short Kindle book allows a writer to keep the project manageable and focused. With a smaller project scope, writers can hone their skills without becoming overwhelmed by a full-length novel or extensive non-fiction book. This approach lends itself to creating a high-quality product in less time, perfect for gaining initial traction and building an audience.

Another advantage of starting with a short Kindle book is the ease and affordability of the publishing process on platforms like Amazon Kindle Direct Publishing (KDP). With KDP, writers are free from traditional gatekeepers and can take full control of their creative projects.

You can set your own prices, access a global audience, and receive a larger share of the royalties compared to traditional publishing methods. Also, the absence of upfront costs allows writers to begin their self-publishing journey with minimal financial risk.

Writing a short Kindle book also provides writers with valuable feedback from readers that can be used to refine and improve future work. This constructive feedback is crucial for growing as a writer and catering to the target audience more effectively.

As a writer gains experience and a stronger understanding of reader preferences, they can confidently move on to larger, more complex projects, knowing that their work will be well-received.

Finally, publishing a short Kindle book can serve as a solid foundation for building a personal brand and a loyal following. Writers can use their initial success as a springboard for future projects, ultimately creating a pipeline of consistent income and a fulfilling writing career.

In summary, writing a short Kindle book is an excellent starting point for writers, allowing for manageable projects, easy and affordable self-publishing, valuable feedback, and brand-building. By starting small and gradually expanding their portfolio, a writer can ensure sustainable growth and long-term success in the self-publishing world.

Here's how to do it:

1. Brainstorm the topic for your book. Make sure it aligns with your message and passion.

2. Outline your book and write it in simple language. Aim for around 30-50 pages to keep it short and accessible.

3. Edit your manuscript and ask a few friends or beta readers for feedback.

4. Create an eye-catching cover and format your book for Kindle.

5. Publish your book on Amazon and promote it on social media, your blog, and email list.

Validation Offer 2. Launch a 4-Week Bootcamp (Coach Influencer)

Are you a coach? A 4-week bootcamp might be the perfect validation offer for you! Launching a 4-week group coaching program is an ideal starting point for coaches looking to expand their practice and build a strong client base. This format offers various benefits, making it an excellent option for new and experienced coaches aiming to create a substantial impact.

First, a 4-week group coaching program is a manageable timeframe that allows the coach to focus on delivering valuable content and guidance without overwhelming participants. The condensed duration fosters a sense of urgency and commitment, motivating clients to actively participate and achieve tangible results. This, in turn, enhances client satisfaction and the likelihood of receiving positive testimonials that can be utilized to attract new clients.

In a group coaching setting, participants benefit from more than just the coach's expertise—they also learn and grow through their peers' shared experiences and insights. This collaborative environment fosters a sense of camaraderie, accountability, and support, further enhancing the program's benefits and perceived value. As a result, the coach can leverage these positive experiences when promoting their services and expanding their reach.

Launching a 4-week group coaching program also enables a coach to maximize their time and impact by serving multiple clients simultaneously. Compared to one-on-one coaching sessions, group programs offer greater efficiency, allowing the coach to increase their overall client load without compromising on the quality and personal attention devoted to each individual. This efficiency can lead to more stable and scalable income streams.

Also, the insights and feedback received throughout the group coaching program can help refine and improve the coach's methodology and approach. By identifying common challenges, pain points, and successes amongst the participants, the coach can continue to develop their skills and offerings, providing even better results for their clients in the future.

Launching a 4-week group coaching program is a perfect place for coaches to start, as it enables them to offer a focused program with tangible results, foster collaboration, and efficiently scale their practice. By continually refining their approach and harnessing the power of group dynamics, coaches can ensure long-term success and positively impact their clients' lives.

Here's how to do it:

1. Decide your bootcamp's focus. Make sure it aligns with your message and passion.

2. Plan weekly content and activities to support participant growth.

3. Outline the benefits and results participants will achieve.

4. Create registration materials and promote your bootcamp to your audience.

5. Run your bootcamp and collect testimonials from satisfied participants.

Validation Offer 3. Create a Mini-Course (Teacher Influencer)

A mini-course can be a fantastic way to share your knowledge if you're a teacher.

Creating a mini-course is the ideal starting point for someone with a teacher influencer voice looking to share their knowledge and expertise with an eager audience. This format offers a host of advantages that make it a fitting option for educators to establish their online presence and kickstart their journey as an influencer.

First, a mini-course's manageable and condensed nature allows a teacher to focus on a specific topic and provide value in an easily digestible format. The bite-sized lessons appeal to a broad audience, including those pressed for time or seeking a quick introduction to a subject. By delivering high-quality content that is both concise and engaging, teachers can quickly build credibility and begin to cultivate a loyal following.

Mini-courses also serve as an excellent testing ground to gauge audience interest and gather feedback for future offerings. As a low-stakes entry point, they allow teachers to experiment with various topics, styles, and formats before investing more time and resources into creating full-length, in-depth courses. This agile approach enables the teacher to adapt and refine their content to resonate better with their target audience over time.

Creating a mini-course can also prove to be beneficial in terms of the teacher's marketing efforts. With a low-cost, high-value offering, attracting potential students and showcasing expertise is easier without a significant upfront commitment. Additionally, the mini-course can serve as an entry point into a funnel that potentially leads to more advanced and higher-priced offerings, effectively nurturing prospective students and monetizing the learning journey.

Finally, a mini-course can be a cornerstone of the teacher's brand, helping them establish a distinct identity in their niche. By weaving in their unique teaching style and voice, they set themselves apart from the competition and foster a strong connection with their audience. As a result, they generate goodwill and credibility that can be leveraged as they continue to evolve their online presence.

In conclusion, creating a mini-course is the perfect starting point for someone with the teacher influencer voice. It allows them to provide focused, high-value content, test audience preferences, support marketing efforts, and build a robust personal brand—all crucial components for long-term success as an online educator and influencer.

Here's how to do it:

1. Decide on the topic for your mini-course, in line with your passion and message.

2. Outline a few short lessons that provide value and actionable tips.

3. Record video lessons or create written modules, depending on your preference.

4. Set up your mini-course on a platform like Gumroad or Kajabi.

5. Promote your mini-course to your audience through social media, blog, and email lists.

Validation Offer 4. Host a 1-Day Virtual Workshop (Speaker Influencer)

For speakers, a 1-day virtual workshop can be an excellent validation offer. It provides a live, interactive experience to share your message and help your audience achieve a specific outcome.

Hosting a 1-day virtual paid workshop is an exceptional starting point for someone with the speaker influencer voice looking to establish their brand and deliver impactful experiences. This engaging and interactive format provides numerous advantages, making it an ideal choice for speakers venturing into the digital space.

First and foremost, a 1-day virtual workshop offers an immersive, focused, and time-limited experience that perfectly suits the speaker's style. The workshop can create an environment that facilitates learning, engagement, and inspiration by combining presentations with practical exercises, activities, and ample opportunities for audience interaction. This deep connection with the audience is pivotal for generating positive word-of-mouth, referrals, and repeat attendees.

Virtual workshops allow speakers to reach a wider audience across geographic boundaries, tapping into a larger and more diverse participant pool. Expanding the reach also enhances the speaker's visibility and awareness, boosting their influence and credibility.

Another advantage of hosting a 1-day virtual workshop as a starting point is its cost-efficiency. Without the need for a physical venue or the added expenses associated with in-person events, speakers can focus on delivering quality content while participants enjoy an accessible and affordable learning opportunity. This low barrier to entry also enables the speaker to attract more attendees, creating greater potential for revenue generation and overall impact.

Gathering feedback during and after the virtual workshop can provide insights into further refining the content and delivery to better resonate with the audience and address their needs. This iterative improvement process is essential to maintaining relevance and encouraging the growth and development of the speaker's unique brand.

Lastly, the momentum and goodwill generated by a successful virtual workshop can lead to an array of opportunities for follow-up activities and programs. From offering exclusive access to presentation recordings to creating advanced workshops, speakers can leverage their workshop's success to expand their offerings, connect with their audience on a deeper level, and continue growing their influence.

In summary, hosting a 1-day virtual paid workshop is an ideal starting point for the speaker influencer voice. It offers an engaging, time-limited experience with broader reach and cost-efficiency while enabling the speaker to gather feedback, improve continuously, and leverage success for future opportunities. As such, it proves to be an effective strategy in building a strong speaker brand and making a lasting impact on the audience.

Here's how to do it:

1. Choose a topic for your workshop that resonates with your message and passion.

2. Plan the workshop's structure, including presentations, activities, and Q&A sessions.

3. Set a date and time for your workshop, and decide on a platform (e.g., Zoom, WebinarJam).

4. Create promotional materials to share with your audience and encourage registration.

5. Run your workshop, engage with your audience, and gather testimonials from satisfied attendees.

As you can see, there are various ways to validate your message and help your target audience. Choose one of these four validation offers, or adapt them to your own unique skills and expertise. The key is to start small and grow your offerings over time. And above all, stay true to your unique message while serving others. Your audience is waiting for you!

In conclusion, selecting the right validation offer is crucial in establishing your presence and making a difference in your target audience's lives. By aligning your chosen validation offer with your unique skills and expertise, you'll effectively test the market, gain valuable insights, and grow your business sustainably and impactfully.

Day 13 Exercise: Select Your Validation Offer

1. Reflect on the four validation offers discussed in this chapter and choose the one that best suits your skills and expertise.

2. Develop a plan for creating and promoting your chosen validation offer.

3. Commit to taking action and implementing your plan, keeping your message and passion at the forefront of your work.

Day 13 Key Takeaways:

- A validation offer is essential for testing your market and determining demand for your product or service.

- It allows you to fine-tune your messaging, build trust and credibility, and minimize upfront investment by starting small.

- Four types of validation offers to consider: write a short Kindle book, launch a 4-week bootcamp, create a mini-course, or host a 1-day virtual workshop.

- Choose the validation offer that aligns with your unique skills, expertise, and passion.

- Commit to taking action and continually refining your offerings to serve your audience and grow your business.

Embarking on your journey with the right validation offer is crucial in finding success and building a loyal following. Focus on staying true to your unique message and serving your audience in a meaningful way, and you'll create a lasting impact and ensure sustainable growth for your business.

14

Day 14. Your Message in a Single Sentence

Did you know that the average attention span of a human has dropped to just eight seconds?[24] Within this brief timeframe, you must seize your audience's attention and convey the essence of your message. With such limited time, it's essential to have a crystal-clear and powerful statement that encapsulates your purpose, target audience, and passion. In this chapter, you'll learn how to formulate a compelling one-sentence message that cuts through the clutter and resonates with your audience.

We'll be diving into a game-changing formula: "I help [people] to [problem/passion] by being a [purpose/strength]." It has the power to define the core of your message, guiding your focus and inspiring your actions as you resonate with your target audience and make a lasting impact in their lives.

Throughout this chapter, we will break down this formula step by step, empower you to identify and understand your audience, nurture your passion for solving a problem, and leverage your unique strengths and purpose. By the end of this journey, you'll possess a one-sentence message that not only serves as your guiding compass but also sets you apart in your industry.

So hold onto your seats, as we embark on an exciting adventure towards a refined, compelling, and impactful one-sentence message that will transform the way you approach your personal and professional life.

Day 14. Define Your Message in a Single Sentence

The one-sentence message formula is an essential method for authors, coaches, speakers, and online business owners to define their message clearly, concisely, and compellingly. Though it may seem simplistic, the formula behind this exercise can yield powerful results when used correctly. Here is the sentence again:

"I help [people] to [problem/passion] by being a [purpose/strength]."

To fully understand how to do the one-sentence exercise effectively, follow these steps:

Part One: Your People (Who Will You Help?)

In chapter six, we guided you through the process of defining your audience by selecting an "egoic label." The concept of the egoic label is drawn from the understanding that people often associate themselves with specific identities that mean something to them. These labels are not meant to pigeonhole people; rather, they help you, as a service provider or business owner, relate with and address the unique needs of your target audience. By choosing an egoic label for your audience, you establish a more profound connection with them and develop a truly tailored message that resonates with their unique circumstances and expectations.

The egoic label you assign to your audience serves as the foundation for your communication and helps you create content that accurately addresses their interests, desires, and struggles. By developing a clear understanding of the people you are trying to reach and the self-identity they embrace, you can design solutions, products, and services that cater specifically to their needs.

Using the egoic label exercise in the earlier chapter, we encouraged you to brainstorm and explore various identities that your prospective audience might adopt. The objective was to help you evaluate different labels and select the one that you believe your audience most strongly identifies with. Furthermore, the exercise aimed to assist you in understanding the mindset and struggles inherent to each label, so you could offer relevant and impactful solutions.

For instance, in my case, I chose the egoic label "overwhelmed messengers" to capture the essence of my audience: writers, speakers, and coaches who often find themselves struggling to navigate the convoluted paths of self-promotion and the sharing of knowledge in a fast-paced, information-saturated world. This label guided my approach to solving their problems by simplifying processes, providing valuable resources, and offering practical solutions.

Part Two: Your Passion (What Problem Will You Solve?)

In chapter ten, we focused on helping you determine the problem you are passionate about solving for your target audience. We posed the question: "What problem are you passionate about solving for the next two to five years?" By addressing this essential question, you can not only identify the issue that resonates with your passion but also align your expertise and professional objectives with the needs of your market.

Identifying a problem that you find genuinely compelling is crucial as it immediately influences your level of dedication, creativity, and energy when developing solutions for your audience. To assist you in finding that passionate problem-solving area, we encouraged you to reflect on your past experiences, skills, interests, and how they could contribute to a specific aspect of your audience's struggles. Additionally, we advised you to consider the long-term perspective and ensure that your chosen problem is sustainable for your business over the years.

Throughout this process, we provided questions and prompts to inspire deep reflection and detailed analysis. As you evaluated various problems, your focus shifted towards the unique value you bring to the table when addressing your target audience's needs. By zeroing in on this passion-fueled problem, you were able to develop a more significant connection with your audience and a profound understanding of their expectations.

For example, in my case, I identified the problem of helping overwhelmed messengers rise above the noise and get paid for what they know. This problem became the central driving force behind my one-sentence message and the solutions I would provide to my audience. Noticing my passion for addressing this issue, I was able to cultivate a clear vision for my business, aiming to create a lasting impact on the lives of my audience.

By answering the question of which problem you are passionate about solving in the earlier chapter, you set the stage for the rest of your messaging and communication efforts. This problem also serves as the crucial component to complete the one-sentence formula for your message, solidifying your commitment to providing value and fostering change for your audience.

Part Three: Your Purpose (How Will You Help Others?)

In chapter five, we guided you through the process of discovering your "hidden superpower" by helping you create a unique combination of two words—your unique gift and your influencer voice. By merging these two elements, you were able to uncover your distinctive edge, setting you apart from others in your field. This hidden superpower not only enhances your abilities to connect and serve your audience but also builds a powerful foundation for your messaging.

To figure out your unique gift, we asked you to reflect on your natural talents, skills, and qualities that distinguish you from others. We encouraged you to consider the attributes you're often praised for or the areas in which you excel with seemingly little effort. This introspection process allowed you to genuinely recognize your strengths and key competencies.

For your influencer voice, we focused on your communication style and the way you convey your message to your audience. By understanding your tone, delivery, and personal approach to sharing your knowledge, you could develop a well-rounded picture of the impact you can create.

Your influencer voice should complement your unique gift, enabling you to establish a consistent, authentic, and relatable image. It also shows you where your core motivations lie. Remember, leaning into your primary influencer voice is your fastest path to impact and income.

Once you identified your unique gift and influencer voice, we showed you how to merge them into your hidden superpower. This superpower, your "two words," provided a concise representation of the distinctive offering you bring to your market.

In my case, my hidden superpower is "resourceful teacher"—a combination of both my innate abilities to provide useful resources and employ an effective teaching style that captures my audience's attention.

By working on uncovering your hidden superpower in the earlier chapter, you laid the groundwork for creating a powerful and compelling one-sentence message.

This superpower plays a critical role in defining your purpose within the one-sentence formula, showcasing how you show up best for your audience, and solidifying your unique, marketable, and impactful brand identity.

Putting it All Together

Defining your message in a single sentence can be enlightening and empowering. By distilling the essence of your purpose, audience, and passion into a concise yet powerful statement, you create a guiding compass for all your efforts, decisions, and actions moving forward. The one-sentence formula is a tool that can help you crystallize your message with focus and impact: "I help [people] to [problem/passion] by being a [purpose/strength]."

To craft your message using the one-sentence formula, begin by reflecting on the three key components:

1. Who are the [people] that you aim to reach and serve? Revisit your target audience, considering the egoic label you established in previous chapters. Be specific and accurate in representing the individuals that make up your intended audience, as this directly impacts the message's resonance and effectiveness.

2. Consider the [problem/passion] that you are fervently committed to solving for your audience. Assess the central issue you identified in the earlier chapter and how your skills, expertise, or unique of-

fering can help overcome it. Ensure that the problem is framed to emphasize your passion and drive to create meaningful change.

3. Reflect on your [purpose/strength], your hidden superpower generated by combining your unique gift and influencer voice. This component is a culmination of your natural abilities and the manner in which you share your message, encapsulating your distinct value to your audience.

With a firm grasp of these components, meld them into the one-sentence formula, delivering a complete statement that reflects who you serve, how you can help them, and how you will effectively achieve it. For instance, my one-sentence message is:

"I help overwhelmed messengers to rise above the noise and get paid for what they know by being a resourceful teacher."

This single-sentence message is not intended to serve as an elevator pitch but as an anchor for clarity and direction in your personal and professional journey. It should clearly understand your audience, your chosen problem to solve, and how your unique strengths and abilities will contribute to your mission. By defining your message in a single sentence using the one-sentence formula, you establish a foundation that drives your purpose, actions, and, ultimately, your success in serving your audience effectively.

My Personal Example

When I embarked on the journey to define my one-sentence message, I knew it would require a deep understanding of my audience, my passion, and my purpose. With these factors in mind, I began to reflect on my experiences, skills, expertise, and core values. The goal was to create a meaningful and powerful statement that captured the essence of what I could offer my audience.

DAY 14. YOUR MESSAGE IN A SINGLE SENTENCE

To begin, I identified my target audience: overwhelmed messengers. These are individuals who often feel inundated by the numerous options they face when carving their path as writers, coaches, and speakers. They struggle with the bombardment of technology, social media, and countless bits of advice from different sources. My mission was to help these overwhelmed messengers focus on the essential aspects of their journey and simplify their approach.

Next, I honed in on the problem I was passionate about solving: helping people rise above the noise and get paid for their knowledge. The "noise" referred to the myriad of distractions and challenges preventing people from achieving their goals. I genuinely cared about assisting my audience in overcoming these odds by leveraging their experiences, skills, and unique knowledge.

Lastly, I contemplated my purpose—how I show up best for my audience. My strengths lie in being a resourceful teacher, providing practical solutions, simplifying complex concepts, and offering actionable advice grounded in my own experiences. My approach to helping overwhelmed messengers is rooted in equipping them with valuable resources and guidance while being a reliable and accessible source of support.

I crafted my one-sentence message with a deep understanding of my audience, passion, and purpose: "I help overwhelmed messengers to rise above the noise and get paid for what they know by being a resourceful teacher." This statement encapsulates the essence of my offering and my unique approach to helping my audience in a way that sets me apart from other professionals in my field.

The process of crafting this one-sentence message was challenging yet rewarding. It served as a continuous reminder of the impact I aimed to create and fostered a clear vision of my purpose, becoming the foundation for my business and my interactions with my audience.

Day 14 Exercise: Crafting Your One-Sentence Message

Set aside 10-15 minutes to complete this exercise. The goal is to create a clear, concise, and powerful one-sentence message that encapsulates your audience, your passion, and your purpose. Follow these steps:

1. Review your previous notes and findings about your target audience, the egoic label you chose, and the problem you are passionate about solving.

2. Reflect on your hidden superpower, considering the combination of your unique gift and influencer voice, and envision how you show up best for your audience.

3. Use the one-sentence formula, "I help [people] to [problem/passion] by being a [purpose/strength]," filling in the blanks with the relevant information from your findings.

4. Write down your one-sentence message and revise it if necessary, ensuring it's clear, concise, and captures the essence of your offering.

5. Reflect on your finished statement, considering how it aligns with your values, goals, and your audience's needs.

Day 14 Key Takeaways:

- A clear, concise message guides your focus and inspires your actions.
- Your target audience, passion-driven problem-solving, and

unique strengths are critical in crafting your one-sentence message.

- The one-sentence formula serves as a foundation for your message: "I help [people] to [problem/passion] by being a [purpose/strength]."

- Developing your one-sentence message provides clarity, direction, and a powerful anchor for your personal and professional journey.

- Consistently revisit and reflect on your one-sentence message to stay focused and aligned with your purpose and audience's needs.

15
The Journey of Discovering Your Message

As we come to the end of Discover Your Message, it's time to reflect on the incredible journey of self-discovery that we've embarked upon together. This book provided you with an opportunity to delve deep into the heart of your purpose and passion, shaping your unique voice in a world that's clamoring for your attention.

The Ignite Your Message Framework introduced you to the methodology that guided your exploration. Through skills assessments, reflective exercises, and mapping out your future, you've gained valuable insights into your inner drive and your influence as a thought-leader in your chosen domain.

Throughout this journey, you've explored the influencer voice assessment, finding the communication style that best suits your personality and resonates with your audience. The one-word exercise helped you sum up your essence and connect with your audience on a deeper level.

The valuable lessons provided in this book revealed the importance of identifying your target audience, understanding their hopes, passions, and struggles. With exercises such as the egoic label, audience filter scorecard, and discovering your audience's goals, you've developed a well-rounded understanding of the people you want to serve.

As you progressed through the chapters, you learned the fundamentals of attracting, engaging, and converting your audience, constructing a strong foundation for growing your platform. You've discovered how to bring people into your world, captivate their interest, and provide them with the support and solutions they need.

Finally, we arrived at the defining moment: consolidating all of the insights gained through this journey into a powerful one-sentence message that perfectly captures your purpose, passion, and the people you are meant to serve.

As you embark on the next phase of your personal and professional path, remember to carry with you the essence of this extraordinary journey. The self-awareness, understanding, and expertise you've cultivated are priceless assets that will set you on the path to a fulfilling and purpose-driven life.

So, hold onto the insights and discoveries made, for they have molded your message as you continue to impact and inspire the lives of those you are destined to serve. Embrace your newfound clarity and confidence, knowing that you've uncovered the essential foundation that will guide you to success and further transform your life and the lives of your audience.

The journey doesn't end here. Remember, the essence of your message resides within you; continue to explore, create, and redefine your narrative, as you share your passion and purpose for the world to see. Let your message shine brightly as you confidently stride towards your destiny, empowering others through your unique voice.

It's time to boldly share your message!

16
The Discover Your Message 14-Day Action Plan

We've been on quite a journey together. But your work is not yet finished.

Finishing a book is great, but applying a book is even better. I don't want you to just move on without applying what you've learned in this book. I believe it has the power to change your life and circumstances.

So, I've decided to take all of the exercises and key takeaways from the book and place them in one convenient place for you.

Use the information below either as a good review or as your personal action plan.

Nothing creates movement like clarity.

If you dedicate a little bit of time to do the exercises and implement what you've learned, your reward will be clarity. From that place of clarity, you can begin to create momentum in your life and business.

This list below is not meant to be a substitute for reading the book. Rather, it is a supplement to helping you integrate what you learned in the book into your business and life.

Let's get started!

Day 1. The Ignite Your Message Framework

The Ignite Your Message Framework consists of purpose, people, and passion. Purpose refers to your unique strengths. People refer to finding your niche audience. Passion refers to finding a specific problem to help your audience solve.

Day 1 Exercise: Reflect on Your Purpose, People, and Passion

- Spend 5-10 minutes journaling about your unique strengths, talents, and abilities. How have you used these in the past to serve others?

- Brainstorm the ideal audience you wish to serve, considering their demographics, desires, pain points, and passions.

- List your areas of interest and expertise, and explore how they align with your audience's needs and your unique talents.

Day 1 Key Takeaways:

- Embrace your unique gifts to enhance your impact and better serve others.

- Define your audience, understanding their needs and desires to foster deep connections.

- Discover and nurture your passion, driving you to help others solve their pressing problems.

Day 2. Finding Your Inner Drive

You are naturally wired in one of four areas: doer, talker, manager, or thinker. The Doer leans toward a coaching role. The Talker leans toward a speaking role. The Manager leans toward a teacher role. The Thinker leans toward a writing role. The 4-part Messenger Interest Grid can help identify which one you primarily are.

Day 2 Exercise: Complete the Messenger Interest Grid Assessment

Take the 4-Part Interest Grid assessment to determine your primary category. It will help you explore your natural interests and potential calling.

Day 2 Key Takeaways:

- The 4-Part Interest Grid comprises the Doer, Manager, Talker, and Thinker.

- Each category has unique traits and helps identify our calling.

- The Doer is task-driven and decisive, while the Manager is detail-oriented and systems-driven.

- The Talker persuades and communicates skillfully, while the Thinker is creative and visionary.

- By identifying which category we fit into, we can discover our calling.

- It's essential to make a decision and go with our gut.

- We can revisit the exercises in this book to see where we end up in the future.

- Clarity comes from movement, and we must approach our work as a calling to find fulfillment.

Day 3. The Influencer Voice Assessment

The Influencer Voice Assessment is a 32-question quiz to help you determine which of four areas of influence your core motivations lie. The four influencer voices are writer, coach, teacher, and speaker. Take the assessment to best determine which influencer voice you should lean into first.

Day 3 Exercise: Discover Your Primary Influencer Voice

- Finish the Influencer Voice Assessment. It reveals your key motivation. Are you a writer, speaker, teacher, or coach?

- Consider how leaning into this primary voice can shape and strengthen your message and impact on your audience.

- Develop a plan to focus on your primary influencer voice for your first (or next) $1,000 earned in your business.

Day 3 Key Takeaways:

- Knowing your influencer voice is vital. It creates an audience connection.

- Focusing on your core motivation will pave the way for a faster income and impact journey.

- Remember that you can develop skills in all four influencer voices as your business grows.

Day 4. Your One Word

Your One Word explains how you show up best for others. Once we understand where our "hidden superpower" lies, we can begin to build a business that adds value to others. We can only discover our one word with the help of others who know us best.

Day 4 Exercise: Find Your One Word

- Compile a list of the five people who know you best.

- Share the Unique Gifts Inventory List with them, asking them to choose five words that best describe you.

- Look for overlapping or similar words and settle on a one-word summary that resonates with your unique self.

- Embrace and celebrate your one-word summary – this is your superpower.

Day 4 Key Takeaways:

- Your unique superpower is the driving force behind your success and impact.

- Understanding and embracing your one word not only refines your message but also provides guidance through life's inevitable changes.

- Seeking input from others can offer valuable insights into finding the essence of your innate strengths.

Day 5. Putting Your Purpose Together

Once you have your primary influencer voice and one word, you can combine the two for a powerful one-two punch. Your two words should give you the confidence to know how you can best build your messenger-based business.

Day 5 Exercise: Create Your Two-Word Purpose

Combine your one-word and primary influencer voice to create a clear and concise purpose statement.

Day 5 Key Takeaways:

- Discovering your gift is essential to finding your purpose.
- Your purpose is not a thing; it's already inside you.
- Your passions may change, but your purpose remains.
- Your purpose is how you show up best for others.
- Listing your one-word and primary influencer voice can help you uncover your purpose.
- Knowing your purpose can help you build a business that aligns with your values and strengths.

Day 6. The Egoic Label Exercise

Egoic labels are labels we like to give ourselves, such as entrepreneur, author, and golfer. One of the best ways to niche down your audience is to find an egoic label to serve. This makes it easier to build a business as we get more acquainted with our egoic label's goals, passions, and struggles.

Day 6 Exercise: The Egoic Label Exercise

Complete the Egoic Label exercise and develop at least four egoic labels you might use to create a business.

Day 6 Takeaways:

- Identifying your specific audience is crucial for the success of your business.

- Use the egoic label exercise to find a self-label that you like.

- Narrow down your audience to a specific group to better understand their needs.

- Identify the problems and challenges that your target audience faces.

- Understand the goals and aspirations of your target audience.

- Know the demographics and psychographics of your target audience.

- Tailor your products and services to the specific needs of your target audience.

- Build a strong relationship with your audience by speaking their language.

Day 7. The Audience Filter Scorecard

Having a hard time narrowing down your audience? That's where the Audience filter Scorecard comes into play. This 6-question scorecard helps you take an analytical approach to identify which audience would be best to build a business on.

Day 7 Exercise: Complete the Audience Filter Scorecard

Complete the Audience Filter Scorecard and narrow your audience to one egoic label.

Day 7 Key Takeaways:

- The audience filter scorecard is a useful tool for identifying your target audience.

- The scorecard helps you to approach audience identification in a logical, step-by-step manner.

- The first step is identifying your egoic label(s), and defining your identity and interests.

- The scorecard asks six questions about your egoic label(s), including whether you enjoy learning about them, whether you are passionate about them, and whether there is a problem to solve for that egoic label.

- Having experience and skills related to your egoic label is an advantage in building a successful business and helps to create valuable content and products.

- Researching other businesses in your field can help you to identify what is working and what can be improved upon and to create a unique value proposition.

- Passion is a powerful force that can drive business success and inspire others.

- While profit-making is important, it should not be the sole focus. The primary focus should be serving your audience and helping them achieve their goals.

- A successful business can be built by identifying a problem and finding a unique solution that resonates with your audience.

Day 8. Discovering Your Audience's Goals

The Audience GPS System is a powerful tool to help you get in the minds of your ideal audience. GPS stands for goals, passions, and struggles. First, we will do a deep dive into uncovering your audience's goals.

Day 8 Exercise: Write Down Your Audience's Goals

Create a list of aspirational goals your ideal customer wants to accomplish based on the research you performed.

Day 8 Key Takeaways:

- Understanding your audience's goals is crucial for creating content and products that resonate with them and building a strong connection.

- Knowing your audience's passions helps you create products and services that resonate with them on a deeper level and build a loyal following.

- Understanding your audience's struggles is critical for creating solutions that meet their needs and provide real value, leading to a loyal customer base and long-term success.

- Historical examples like Henry Ford demonstrate the importance of understanding your audience's struggles and addressing them effectively.

- By understanding your audience's goals, passions, and struggles, you can identify new opportunities for growth and innovation, stay ahead of the curve, and position your business for continued success.

Day 9. Finding Your Audience's Passions

When you align yourself with your audience's passions, you build trust with them. Passions might be related to values, worldviews, perspectives, or unique points of view.

A great example is the FIRE community in the world of finance, which stands for Financial Independence, Retire Early. Their community values simple, frugal living that is counter-culture to how most Americans live today.

Day 9 Exercise: Measure Your Audience's Passion (and Enthusiasm)

- Go to Google Trends and search for your niche or sub-niche. Set the timeframe to the past year or five years.

- Compare your search results to those of established or popular niches to determine consistency and potential profitability.

- Explore LinkedIn and Facebook groups related to your niche, paying attention to the frequency and enthusiasm of posts and discussions.

Day 9 Key Takeaways:

- Google Trends is a powerful tool for measuring consistency and potential profitability in your chosen niche.

- Comparing your search results to proven niches can help you determine the consistency of your chosen sub-niche - and whether it's worthy of investing time and effort.

- Beware of fads - focus on passions that have proven sustainability rather than short-lived crazes.

- Social networking platforms like LinkedIn and Facebook groups offer invaluable insights into audience enthusiasm and networking opportunities.

Day 10. Uncovering Your Audience's Struggles

Every successful business solves problems. Once you know your audience's struggles, you'll know how to best help them.

People pay money to solve their problems.

One of the best ways to see if our niche can be profitable is by performing market research online. The good news is you don't need a bachelor's degree in business to do effective market research.

Let's look at some free tools we can use online to find out if the niche we've chosen will be profitable before we even get started.

Day 10 Exercise: Action Steps for Your Income Streams

1. Head over to Amazon, search for eBooks, print books, and audiobooks related to your niche, and analyze customer behavior by examining reviews and sales rankings.

2. Browse Clarity.fm to find coaches within your niche, looking for reviews, ratings, and engagement and determining if their offerings align with yours.

3. Research courses on Udemy.com related to your niche, examining factors like reviews, ratings, and student engagement.

4. Use Google to search for conferences, workshops, or associations relevant to your niche, and take note of the speaking opportunities that catch your attention.

Day 10 Key Takeaways:

- Utilize Amazon to explore the demand for eBooks, print books, and audiobooks in your niche, informing your decision on which products to create.

- Confirm the demand for coaching services within your niche by leveraging Clarity.fm, ensuring that your audience is willing to pay for your guidance.

- Use Udemy.com to examine the potential for creating online courses and memberships that cater to your audience's preferred topics.

- Employ Google to unlock speaking opportunities by searching for niche conferences and events where you can share your expertise and build your reputation.

Day 11. Awareness: How Will I Attract Them?

To build a successful business online, you need to create awareness. Most people try to create awareness by promoting themselves over and over again. A more powerful way to build awareness for your brand is by creating valuable content in the form of blogs, podcasts, and YouTube videos.

Day 11 Exercise: How Will You Attract Your Audience?

Your Day 11 exercise is choosing whether to launch a blog, podcast or YouTube channel. But what if you want to choose more than just one? For now, select the one content channel that best aligns with your influencer voice. You can always expand your reach later by launching one of the other two.

Day 11 Key Takeaways:

- Building awareness is essential for sharing your message, and choosing the right platform can greatly impact your success.

- Blogging is a timeless and powerful platform to share your message through writing, with a focus on consistency, quality, and promotion.

- Podcasting provides an intimate connection by allowing your audiences to engage with your voice, offering unique insights, and becoming a respected voice in your niche.

- YouTube delivers a rich, engaging experience by combining visual, auditory, and emotional elements, creating a memorable connection with your viewers.

- Regardless of the platform you choose, prioritize creating valuable content, engaging with your audience, and adopting effective promotion strategies for maximum impact.

Day 12. Engagement: How Will I Capture Them?

Once you've successfully captured the attention of your audience, now what? The next step is to build an ongoing relationship with them. The best way to do this is by building an email list. The relationship is in the email list, and the money is in the relationship. People buy from people they know, like, and trust. Let's take a closer look at some of the best ways to build an email list.

Day 12 Exercise: Come Up with Your Lead Magnet

Brainstorm a list of two or three potential lead magnet ideas, such as eBooks, guides, checklists, or exclusive video content that would appeal to your target audience.

Day 12 Key Takeaways:

- Email lists allow you to communicate directly with your audience, maintaining control of your message and fostering personal connections.

- Building an email list boosts sales and strengthens your credibility as an author, coach, or speaker.

- Utilize lead magnets and strategic calls-to-action to encourage sign-ups across different platforms.

- Regularly produce valuable content that resonates with your audience and continually promotes your email list.

- Embrace collaborations with others in your niche to expand your reach and attract new subscribers.

- Monitor and analyze your email list growth and engagement to continually optimize your strategies for success.

Day 13. Conversion: How Will I Help Them?

Once you have a targeted list of email subscribers, you can begin to monetize your list. But how do you know what they will pay money for? That's where validation offers come into play.

Validation offers allow you to test the waters before you spend time building something no one wants. Validation offers allow you to sell before you create. The good news is there are validation offers you can employ for every influencer voice: writer, coach, teacher, and speaker.

Day 13 Exercise: Select Your Validation Offer

1. Reflect on the four validation offers discussed in this chapter and choose the one that best suits your skills and expertise.

2. Develop a plan for creating and promoting your chosen validation offer.

3. Commit to taking action and implementing your plan, keeping your message and passion at the forefront of your work.

Day 13 Key Takeaways:

- A validation offer is essential for testing your market and determining demand for your product or service.

- It allows you to fine-tune your messaging, build trust and credibility, and minimize upfront investment by starting small.

- Four types of validation offers to consider: write a short Kindle book, launch a 4-week bootcamp, create a mini-course, or host a 1-day virtual workshop.

- Choose the validation offer that aligns with your unique skills, expertise, and passion.

Day 14. Define Your Message in a Single Sentence

Let's boil all of our hard work down to a single sentence. This one-sentence message will easily communicate the three-part Ignite Your Message Framework: purpose, people, and passion. Your one sentence will help you create a memorable statement reminding you how you show up best for others.

Day 14 Exercise: Crafting Your One-Sentence Message

Set aside 10-15 minutes to complete this exercise. The goal is to create a clear, concise, and powerful one-sentence message that encapsulates your audience, your passion, and your purpose. Follow these steps:

1. Review your previous notes and findings about your target audience, the egoic label you chose, and the problem you are passionate about solving.

2. Reflect on your hidden superpower, considering the combination of your unique gift and influencer voice, and envision how you show up best for your audience.

3. Use the one-sentence formula, "I help [people] to [problem/passion] by being a [purpose/strength]," filling in the blanks with the relevant information from your findings.

4. Write down your one-sentence message and revise it if necessary, ensuring it's clear, concise, and captures the essence of your offering.

5. Reflect on your finished statement, considering how it aligns with your values, goals, and your audience's needs.

Day 14 Key Takeaways:

- A clear, concise message guides your focus and inspires your actions.

- Your target audience, passion-driven problem-solving, and unique strengths are critical in crafting your one-sentence message.

- The one-sentence formula serves as a foundation for your message: "I help [people] to [problem/passion] by being a [purpose/strength]."

- Developing your one-sentence message provides clarity, direction, and a powerful anchor for your personal and professional journey.

- Consistently revisit and reflect on your one-sentence message to stay focused and aligned with your purpose and audience's needs.

Thank You

I want to express my gratitude for choosing and purchasing my book. In a world overflowing with choices, you selected mine, and for that, I'm truly thankful.

Before we part ways, may I request a minor favor? Would it be too much to ask for you to leave a review on the platform? For an independent author like myself, receiving direct reader feedback through reviews significantly contributes to the success of the work.

Your insights will guide me in creating content that effectively aids you in achieving your desired results. Your feedback is highly valuable to me. Thank you for your time and consideration.

Leave a review by going to: **JMill.Biz/Discover-Review**

1. Stearns, Richard. Unfinished: Believing is Only the Begin-ning. United States: Thomas Nelson, 2013.

2. Adams, Susan. "Most Americans Are Unhappy At Work." Forbes, June 20, 2014. https://www.forbes.com/sites/susanadams/2014/06/20/most-americans-are-unhappy-at-work/?sh=2a78168b341a. Accessed August 8, 2023.

3. Leider, Richard J, and David A Shapiro. Whistle While You Work: Heeding Your Life's Calling. [PDF] Accessed August 8, 2023.

4. Dixon, Brian. Start with Your People: The Daily Decision that Changes Everything. United States: Zondervan, 2019.

5. "Declaration for John F. Kennedy Space Center." NASA. Accessed August 8, 2023. https://history.nasa.gov/moondec.html.

6. "Unlock the Power of Purpose." Richard Leider. Accessed August 8, 2023. https://richardleider.com/unlock-the-power-of-purpose/

7. Schawbel, Dan. "Evan Carmichael: How To Define Your Life Purpose In One Word." Forbes, December 9, 2016. https://www.forbes.com/sites/danschawbel/2016/12/09/evan-carmichael-how-to-define-your-life-purpose-in-one-word/?sh=b49897c2a0ea. Accessed August 8, 2023.

8. Barysevich, Aleh. "How Social Media Influence 71% Consumer Buying Decisions." Search Engine Watch, November 20, 2020. https://www.searchenginewatch.com/2020/11/20/how-social-media-influence-71-consumer-buying-decisions/.

9. Kurichenko, Victoria. "Consumers Do Not Buy What You Do, They Buy Why You Do It." Publicist, no date. https://www.publicist.co/the-spin/the-inside-scoop/consumers-do-not-buy-what-you-do-they-buy-why-you-do-it#:~:text=As%20Simon%20Sinek%20well%2Dsaid,that%20prove%20what%20they%20believe.%E2%80%9D

10. "Meaning and Purpose: What's the Difference" Vic Strecher. Accessed August 8, 2023. https://online.umich.edu/collections/future-of-teaching/short/meaning-and-purpose-whats-the-difference/

11. Earley, Daphne. "Finding Purpose in Your Career: Tips for Building a Meaningful Professional Life." *LinkedIn*, 6 Mar. 2019, www.linkedin.com/pulse/finding-purpose-your-career-tips-building-meaningful-daphne-earley/. Accessed 31 Jul. 2023.

12. Library of Congress. "This Month in Business History: Coca Cola is First Served in May." *Library of Congress*, 2023, www.guides.loc.gov/this-month-in-business-history/may/coca-cola-first-served. Accessed 31 Jul. 2023.

13. Zhu, Lily. "Blogging Businesses Experience 126% Higher Lead Growth Than Non-Blogging Businesses." *HubSpot*, 27 Jan. 2010, www.blog.hubspot.com/blog/tabid/6307/bid/5519/blogging-businesses-experience-126-higher-lead-growth-than-non-blogging-businesses.aspx. Updated 18 Oct. 2015. Accessed 31 Jul. 2023.

14. "Lisa. 'Warby Parker: Disrupting the Eyewear Industry.' TECHNOLOGY AND OPERATIONS MANAGEMENT, December 12, 2015. https://d3.harvard.edu/platform-rctom/submission/warby-parker-disrupting-the-eyewear-industry/."

15. Mintel. 'Seven in 10 Americans Seek out Opinions Before Making Purchases.' Mintel, 3 June 2015, https://www.mintel.com/press-centre/seven-in-10-americans-seek-out-opinions-before-making-purchases/.

16. Ford Motor Company. 'The Moving Assembly Line and The Five-Dollar Workday.' Ford Motor Company, 2020, https://corporate.ford.com/articles/history/moving-assembly-line.html.

17. Kwok, Preston. 'e-Learning Industry Report.' Grow Enrollments, 2023, https://growenrollments.com/education-center/e-learning-industry-report/.

18. Shaw, George Bernard. 'The single biggest problem in communication is the illusion that it has taken place.' BrainyQuote, 2023, https://www.brainyquote.com/quotes/george_bernard_shaw_385438.

19. "Lieberman, Mike. '10 Stats About Inbound Marketing That Will Make Your Jaw Drop.' HubSpot, 2023, https://blog.hubspot.com/insiders/inbound-marketing-stats."

20. "Gray, Colin. 'Podcast Industry Stats' The Podcast Host, 2023, https://www.thepodcasthost.com/listening/podcast-industry-stats/"

21. "McLachlan, Stacey. 'How the YouTube Algorithm Works' HootSuite, 2023, https://blog.hootsuite.com/how-the-youtube-algorithm-works/."

22. Zhou, Luisa. 'Email Marketing ROI Statistics.' Luisa Zhou, 2023, https://www.luisazhou.com/blog/email-marketing-roi-statistics/."

23. "Bryant, Sean. 'How Many Startups Fail and Why.' Investopedia, 2022, https://www.investopedia.com/articles/personal-finance/040915/how-many-startups-fail-and-why.asp."

24. "Ranieri & Co Staff Writer, 'Changing Attention Span and What it Means for Content.' Ranieri & Co, 2021, https://www.ranieriandco.com/post/changing-attention-span-and-what-it-means-for-content-in-2021."

Printed in Great Britain
by Amazon